Tom,

Enjoy the history of Masontown!

Bar Mh

MASONTOWN
FRISCO'S VICTORIA MINE
&
GHOST TOWN

MASONTOWN
FRISCO'S VICTORIA MINE
&
GHOST TOWN

Blair Miller

FRISCO HISTORIC PARK
AND MUSEUM PRESS
120 E. Main Street
Frisco, Colorado 80443

Published in the United States of America by
Frisco Historic Park and Museum Press
120 E. Main Street
Frisco, Colorado 80443
www.friscohistoricpark.com

Masontown
Frisco's Victoria Mine & Ghost Town

Blair Miller

1st edition: June 1, 2022

ISBN: 978-1-943829-44-6

Library of Congress Control Number: 2022908524

PRINTED IN THE UNITED STATES OF AMERICA

Cover concept - Blair Miller   Cover design - Donald Kallaus
Book design/layout - Suzanne Schorsch

Cover photographs: Top - Frisco residents outside of a cabin at Masontown, c. 1910.
(Frisco Historic Park & Museum)
Bottom - The Empty Grade for Masontown Mill, © 2021 Blair Miller

Hiking Guide illustrations by Amber Zundel
Frisco Historic Park and Museum Press is an imprint of Rhyolite Press LLC

To Colorado's first people, the Ute, the men and women who withstood mountain hardships to build a life for themselves amongst this range, and the hundreds of unnamed miners who worked ceaselessly in the hidden tunnels of Summit County that have since collapsed. Researching and writing this book would not have been possible without the guidance that I have received throughout my career from mentors, along with my partner Shelby, and the dozens of other friends and family who have accompanied me to the old site of Masontown countless times for research, inspiration, and recreation.

Contents

Preface

Just outside of Frisco and halfway up Mount Royal, hikers will find themselves walking through a flush section of the mountain. They may see brick foundations, with scattered, rusted, pieces of metal lining the trails. Pairing to the side of this flat section, a large avalanche scar follows from here leading atop Victoria Mountain. This area currently serves as a pleasant break from the incline of the Mount Royal trail, but once held a different purpose. The few remains that are seen today offer a glimpse into the past and tell the story of this mountain.

This section of the property, given the name Masontown, is one of the most arguable parts of Frisco's history. Differing stories offer entirely different timelines and functions of this camp that grew around the Victoria mine. The alternating accounts of what transpired here have led to a general mystery of the rise and fall of this mining camp.

As the story goes, the Victoria mine originally began in the mid-1860s, nearly 15 years before Frisco was a town. A large strike at the Victoria was quickly followed by the involvement of an investor named General Napoleon Bonaparte Buford, who is said to have built a mill then left town shortly after. From there, it turned into the Masontown property, owned and operated by the Masontown Mining and Milling

Company in the early 1870s. Under this ownership, the property held a mill, several cabins, and a boarding house. The operations here ended after a snow slide on New Year's Eve, of 1911, leaving the remains as a ghost town. Another slide struck in 1926, completely decimating the once booming camp. Stories mention moonshiners that worked out of the abandoned property during prohibition, seeking the same desire for riches that drove its first investors to the area. Removal of the dilapidated structures that remained after several snow slides took place in the late 1960s, leaving behind only the fragments that are seen today.

Some accounts note that Masontown once held a population of several hundred, which would have rivaled the still growing population of Frisco at the time. Others say that no more than 30 people ever lived there concurrently. Some even argue that it was never truly a populated town, but instead, a few scattered buildings and cabins, with the mines' workers commuting from Frisco.

One thing could be known for sure, there was a mine here that saw enough success to draw in company investors.

The perseverance, determination, and hardship endured by those involved here prove true to that of Frisco's first townsfolk, with the Victoria's story demonstrating the true spirit of early settlements in the Rocky Mountain West.

The objective of this book is to analyze the primary sources, such as mining claims, deeds, journals, letters, directories, and newspapers, of the time to portray a full view of this property throughout the years. While oral histories and local stories are not disputed, they will be looked at through a new lens, shining a light on some of the details that may have been forgotten as time progressed, and as result, relaying a more complete history of the importance behind this property.

A drawn map of all lodes and claims relating to this property is included on page 81. A glossary of mining terms used throughout this book is included on page 83, and a time line of major events related to this property is on page 87.

A General Mix Up

The story of the Masontown property begins with General Napoleon Bonaparte (N.B.) Buford. As it is told, General Buford invested in the recently opened Victoria mine that sat on current Mount Royal in either 1865 or 1866. Being a mine developer, Buford built a mill and funded further exploration into this lode. After not receiving the timely payout that he desired, Buford left town, taking his investments with him. He was never again to be heard from in the area soon to become Frisco.

Napoleon Bonaparte Buford was born in Woodford, Kentucky, in 1807, to plantation owners John and Nancy Hickman Buford. As Napoleon came of age, he followed his namesake in pursuing a military career, graduating from West Point Academy in 1827 and serving in the army for the next eight years. In the mid-1830s, he retired from the military into an engineering job for a railroad company in Illinois, eventually working his way up to company president. Upon the seeding of the American Civil War, Buford reentered the military and climbed the ranks resulting in his eventual promotion to Union Brigadier General.

In 1861, he led an infantry unit in the Battle of Belmont as Colonel of the 27th Illinois Infantry. The following year after being promoted to Brigadier General, Buford commanded the 1st Brigade, 3rd Division, at the Battle of Corinth. Despite his dedication throughout the war, Napoleon never received the same acclaim as his half-brother, famed John Buford, who is known for his crucial efforts at the Battle of Gettysburg.

General Napoleon Bonaparte Buford.
(Library of Congress)

After finishing his service with the Union Army in 1865, Buford headed west and began a career in Colorado. He settled in Idaho Springs, sitting roughly 30 miles west of Denver, and resorted back to his engineering skillset. After their incorporation on March 27, 1866, Buford served as the Superintendent for the Federal Union Mining Company of Colorado. His duties under this position were to scout and develop promising mining ventures surrounding the town.

That following spring, after a short term of his position, General Buford was let go from his title after the company's Board of Directors expressed their displeasure with Buford's management of claims. With no mining company looking to hire him after consulting with his former employer, he took his engineering skills to another growing industry in the Rocky Mountain West, the railroads. Buford began work with the Union Pacific Railroad in 1867 serving as government inspector to the company for the following two years. While working for this railroad, Buford also served as special commissioner of Indian Affairs from 1867 to 1868.

After several unsuccessful attempts to establish himself out west, he eventually returned to Illinois. Buford died in Chicago in April of 1883.

While N.B. Buford can be placed in Colorado and around mining developments in the late 1860s, he cannot be placed directly in Summit County. His office for the Federal Union Mining Company, however, was in the neighboring county of Clear Creek.

Throughout his time working for this mining syndicate, Buford invested in and located dozens of mines on the company's behalf, including one called the Victoria. Sharing the same name as Masontown's future lode, this Victoria sat just south of Idaho Springs, roughly forty miles from present-day Frisco.

Along with developing this Victoria mine, south of Idaho Springs, Buford also built a bridge to cross the creek and several buildings on the immediate property. Of the largest was a 50 by 70-foot wooden mill, which Buford named after himself. Alongside his mill construction, he cut a large race, an open ditch to redirect water, to run the river toward his mine. The race then dropped its stream onto a large turbine wheel, harnessing its water-power for milling. The Buford Mill processed ores with ten arrastras, a spun cylinder that would crush and pulverize ores as they slowly dragged along the bottom aside wooden planks. While the use of arrastras was fading as mining technologies improved, Buford utilized them at his mill as they required little maintenance and cost once assembled.

While there were dozens of mines named Victoria throughout Colorado in the nineteenth century, with several of them being within forty miles of Frisco, this is the only one to have its pairing mill hold the name "Buford Mill."

A camp soon grew around this mine and property in Clear Creek County. Following the success of its ore return and milling operations, this mining camp began making newspaper headlines by the late 1860s. The name given to this camp surrounding the Victoria mine and Buford Mill was Masonville, after A. S. Mason, an owner of the company.

After a reduced to abandoned workforce on behalf of the Federal Union Mining Company and General Buford, the Franklin Company purchased the property and built a new mill over the old Buford Mill in 1871. At this time, the Federal Union Mining Company began to slacken in the state of Colorado and officially ceased operations in 1875.

While it cannot be ruled out that General Buford did the same in Frisco as in Idaho Springs, there are no primary sources that can prove he was the first investor of the future Masontown property. However, the two stories do strike several similarities. When told in chronological order, the Idaho Springs story sounds identical to the previous story of the beginning of Frisco's Masontown.

> A company led by General Buford invested in a Victoria Mine in 1866, which sat just outside of the town. He then built a "Buford Mill" and abandoned the claim shortly after. A large syndicate next purchased the mine in the early 1870s and rebuilt the mill.

As to add more to the similarities, the names of the camps that surrounded both Victoria mines strike eerily close, from Masontown to Masonville.

The 1867 edition of *The Mines of Colorado*, only reported one company to be operating in this section of the Tenmile mining district, in which Frisco was located. This company was the Whitney & Whiting Co., headed by Superintendent A.A. Sawyer. Their prize lode, however, was located south of Frisco near Fletcher Mountain, named the Capitol Lode.

Furthermore, Stanley Dempsey, once a lawyer of the Climax Mine, noted in his writings that there was only one habitable cabin in the Tenmile District at the beginning of 1878. He goes on to explain that many surrounding towns and camps were established mere months into 1879.

It is possible that as time passed and the legend of Masontown grew, the similarities between the Victoria nearing Frisco and the Masonville nearing Idaho Springs blended to become how we hear about the founding of this property today.

The Founding of a Town

In the early 1870s, a man by the name of Henry Recen made his way to the tenmile Canyon in search of mining riches. With nearby Breckenridge attracting miners as early as 1859, many prospectors had traveled through soon to become Frisco on their journey to the growing gold town, but never stopped to investigate the mountains this far to the north.

Henry Recen (Frisco Historic Park & Museum)

Recen, originally from Sweden, built a cabin in town in 1873, and began mining. This resulted in him opening Frisco's first silver lode, named the Juno, which sat on the west face of Mount Royal roughly 100 feet above the valley floor. Following successful silver returns, Recen realized that he had exceeded the amount of work he could put into this venture alone, and returned home to Sweden in an attempt to bring his family back to Colorado with him. While he was away in 1876, Capt. Henry Learned placed a sign on the Recen cabin reading "Frisco City".

The name "Frisco", nevertheless, was not chosen at random. While making that sign, Learned was thinking about the future of Summit County and how he can connect this area with the growing world. The name he had chosen was a direct ploy to bring in an expanding railroad line, figuring that having this route coming through Frisco would create an economy in the valley. The Frisco Line that Learned wanted to draw in was named as an acronym for the San Francisco (FR) & Saint Louis (IS) Railroad Company (CO). Learned's efforts did not return his hopes, as this line never ran through the area and instead was routed to Frisco, Texas. Despite no railroad arrival on behalf of the Frisco Line, the name for this new town founded by Recen stuck.

Upon his return, Henry Recen, accompanied by his brothers Daniel and Andrew, began locating mines throughout the Tenmile Canyon, focusing in greatly on Mount Royal. Along with him being credited as Frisco's founder, Henry and his brothers held pivotal in the creation of other towns in the area, such as Kokomo, Robinson, and Recen.

With its perfect placement between the mining hotspots of Georgetown and Leadville, Frisco grew into a halfway stop, first serving carriages. Many travelers noticed the potential of establishing themselves in this area that appeared to show nothing but growth. One of these interested individuals was Peter Leyner, who moved to town in 1879 and opened the Leyner Hotel on Main Street. This hotel boasted two floors, housing six rooms and a cellar on the first, and eleven rooms on the second. In the back of the hotel, Leyner had built a stable and livery to aid the carriage route that passed through. Leyner, however, held more interest in being a hotel owner instead of maintaining a hotel, and the hotel began to degrade without proper care that led to a roof cave-in in 1887.

By the year 1880, Frisco had officially been incorporated as a town and was listed in the Colorado State Directory. Main Street hosted several stores, multiple hotels and saloons, and a post office, with the town's population nearing 250 citizens. The many mines surrounding the area and the workforce that they employed held responsible for the population growth that developed into a town charter.

Leyner Hotel, c. 1889 (Frisco Historic Park & Museum)

The next developmental step for the growth and attraction to Frisco was to ease transportation to this town. Two railroads would soon enter the area fueled by this purpose, being the Denver & Rio Grande (D&RG) opening in 1882, and the Denver, South Park, & Pacific Railroad (DSP&PRR) opening in 1883. Both of these railroads were narrow-gauge, meaning that their tracks were closer together than an average railway. This would aid them in carving through the twists and turns necessary to maneuver mountain passes. While the D&RG ran directly through town on the current alleyway between Main Street and Galena Street, the DSP&PRR followed the outside of town and wrapped around the Tenmile Range on what is currently the Recreation Path. Given the heavyweights of ore that their trains would transport on the elevation battling tracks, the DSP&PRR was given the nickname, "Damn Slow Pulling & Pretty Rough Riding."

Shortly after incorporation of the town, Frisco was branded with a name that could have served detrimental to its growth: the town where you can get away with murder.

As the sun began to rise on the morning of Thursday, October 20, 1881, Frisco townsfolk made their way over dirt roads into town to start their day. Looking for breakfast and a coffee, a few of them headed for Morrow S. S. Saloon, situated on Main Street near the Leyner Hotel and the Frisco Lodge. Confusion struck these citizens as they noticed that the saloon had not yet been opened as it was every morning at 5:00 am. James McWalters, the proprietor and bartender of the establishment, was known for having his doors open early every morning to serve the miners as they made their way to work. To add to this confusion, his lantern on the front door had been left out from the night before. As they began to pound on the entrance door and call out for McWalters, they were met with no response. The curious patrons made their way to the back door and found that it was not only unlocked but also left halfway open. As the men entered the saloon, they noticed McWalters' body lying on the floor. One of his usual customers had assumed that McWalters had too much to drink the night before and propped him upright, shaking him and yelling to wake him up. As he noticed the markings on McWalters' face and the blood underneath his body, it became apparent that he was talking to a dead man.

Upon realizing that a foul deed had taken place, the men who had discovered McWalters' body began looking around the saloon for anything that would assist in naming a suspect. Laying on the billiards table near McWalters' body, they found a pocketknife covered in blood. Alongside this knife were drops of blood, staining the green felt. Behind the bar, they found a dirk with a fawn's foot handle, although no blood was near this dagger. A second dirk was found just outside the back door. Scratching and shuffling marks in the ground surrounded this knife as if somebody had dropped it and tried to recover the weapon through the dark of night.

James McWalters was a 45-year-old man and considered to be

universally liked by the people of Frisco. Born in England in 1836, he spent years in the service of the British Army. In early 1881, McWalters moved to Summit County and later settled in Frisco. His demise followed shortly after moving to the town, as he had only been living in Frisco for a few weeks to assume his role as saloon proprietor.

Initial reports had believed that McWalters was shot with a revolver, brought to light from a local constable. As gossip spread around town, the reasoning for the fight became understood that the patrons wanted a drink, yet had no money to pay for one. After spending all of their money on gambling, McWalters offered to cover the cost of one round to put the tensions of these railroad workers at ease. After they finished their free drinks, McWalters strictly enforced that there would be no more drinks without paying for them. The response of his guests was unsettling, stating that they would have either whiskey or blood.

As the investigation continued, those in search of the assailant, or assailants, were led to the workers of the Denver & Rio Grande Railroad. All workers of this line had just received their long-awaited time checks, and as usual, they intended on spending them on a night of drinking and gambling. The *Leadville Weekly Democrat* reported on the events that surrounded Frisco on this payday, stating, "The peace of the town was knocked into a cocked hat by the hideous carousals of the discharged laborers, and there was not one who wouldn't have thrown dice for a square meal or a drink of vile liquor." As most of the townsfolks turned in for the night, they noted that many of the Irish workers of the railroad had left for Morrow S. S. Saloon to continue with their evening. Immediate thoughts were that a country feud between the Irish workers and British McWalters had led to his death. To further support this theory, two of the knives that had been recovered were recognized as belonging to Irish workers of the railroad company.

The next morning, Summit County Deputy Sherriff George Chase arrived in Frisco via train to investigate further into the murder on Main Street. Chase had recently brought fugitive J.H. Cramer to justice after killing police officer Joe Morgan and had hoped to bring the same fate to those responsible for McWalters death. He issued a warrant out for John Hopkins and Terrance Johnson, based on the identification of two of the knives being theirs.

Hopkins was spotted shortly after in nearby Robinson and arrested on the charges of being associated with McWalters murder. While in custody, he refused to give a statement on the affair, enraging the locals. As tensions rose, citizens of Robinson started demanding that Hopkins be hung from a tree to scare his testimony out of him. To prevent the local mob from having their way, Hopkins was placed under a twenty-four hour watch in the Robinson Jail.

As several days passed, the physicians working on McWalters' death determined what it was that had ended his life. After observing the marking on his face, they devised that he was not shot, but received his fatal wound from a blow to the temple. As the full scope of this crime fell into light following physicians releasing this statement, an awaited testimony on behalf of Hopkins came to the surface as well.

Late Thursday night, October 27, Hopkins broke his silence and released a voluntary statement revealing what had truly transpired the week before. Hopkins told that he and his former partner at the railroad company, James Driscoll, were returning to their cabin on the outskirts of town from a night of drinking. As they passed by Morrow S. S. Saloon, they decided to stop in and attempt to gamble in exchange for drinks. They proposed this offer to McWalters, insisting that he join them for a hand. McWalters sat at the table, with only Hopkins and Driscoll in the bar, and began dealing. Several hands were played, all resulting in favor of McWalters. This lack of luck enraged Driscoll, leading to his claim of McWalters being a cheat. As verbal exchanges escalated, Driscoll reached for his Winchester rifle seated beside him. He leaped towards McWalters, striking him in the head with the stock of his rifle and knocking him down, resulting in instant death. Driscoll immediately sprung up and ran towards the back door, with Hopkins in pursuit.

Following this statement, an investigation into Driscoll ensued. The police intercepted a package at the Breckenridge post office, labeled, "James Driscoll to James Driscoll. Denver, Colorado." Inside this package, they found the fore mentioned Winchester rifle, stained in blood. The Denver post office never reported James coming in for this baggage, leading Sheriff Chase and his associates to believe Driscoll intended to distract them from his true location.

James Driscoll managed to evade the law chasing after him. Many believed that Driscoll had run to hide in one of the neighboring mining towns, as he had recently taken up prospecting after his release from the Denver & Rio Grande Railroad Company. John Hopkins was charged with being an accessory to the murder of James McWalters but was released on bond after giving his testimony.

Only a few years into its existence, the sprouting town of Frisco had made a name for itself in both mountain communities and national mining cohorts. Not only did it prove that it had the minerals necessary for large operations, but it also demonstrated a willing workforce, the infrastructure necessary to house them, and the means to transport both workers and ore back down the mountains to Denver.

FRISCO.

Mining town in Summit County. Population 250. Daily mails and stages to Georgetown and Breckenridge. Distances: Breckenridge, 10 miles; Leadville, 25; Georgetown, 35; Como, 27; Kokomo, 15; Red Cliff, 22.

FRISCO BUSINESS DIRECTORY.

Ballif, Adolph, blacksmith.
Canon Hotel, H. Stafford, propr.
Clinton, J. J., hotel.
Colomar Mining Co., R. B. Weiser, supt.
Crowell, D. C., clerk and constable.
Evans, W. H., postmaster.
Evans, Wm. H. & Son, groceries.
Erank, J. J., saloon.
Frisco Mining & Discovery Co., Wm. Fletcher, sec'y.
Frisco Hotel, J. J. Clinton, propr.
Garretson, John, assayer.
Graff, A. C., mayor.
High Line Stages, daily.
Hunter, John, marshal.
Leyner Hotel, H. C. Babcock, propr.
Learned, Henry, notary and justice of peace.
Mensch, W. A., notary.
Morris, R., physician.
Morrow, S. S., saloon.
Royal Mt. M. & M. Co., C. S. Thompson, manager.
Scott, J. S., groceries and miners' supplies.
Shedd, C. F., lumber mill, J. W. Graveline, manager.
Smith, Frank, news-dealer, candies, etc.
Smith, Isador, barber.
Thompson, Chas. S., groceries, feed, etc.
Weiser, R. B., physician.
Whipp, C. J., laundry.

1882 Colorado State Directory, Frisco Listing. The Morrow Saloon, along with Leyner Hotel and many other businesses are listed.
(Frisco Historic Park & Museum)

The Royal Mountain

The incorporation of Frisco, along with its expanding economy and two railroads moving through town, led to more publicity of the happenings in Frisco. Local newspapers had dedicated sections to this growing boomtown, such as "Frisco Facts" or "Frisco Items". The *Leadville Weekly Democrat*, a popular newspaper of the time from nearby Leadville, reported a six-inch streak of good ore at the Victoria under their "Frisco Facts" section. This report on July 10, 1880, was the first published account of the Frisco's Victoria mine.

Similar news of the many successful strikes near Frisco began to spread, resulting in the attention of investors from all around aiming towards this area and its possibilities. Three of the investors who took notice to these happenings were Messrs. Alex C. Graff, his brother William M. Graff, and William McNair. The Graff brothers were originally from Pennsylvania, and now lived at Kokomo, a mining town just up the Tenmile Canyon from Frisco. They had invested in a small number of mines throughout the Tenmile Canyon, and had their sights set on expanding their ownership and operations. Chasing their desire for expansion, the Graffs and partner McNair traveled to Frisco in early 1880.

They began evaluating the local Frisco mines and land plots with the intention of building a smelter and further developments. After several promising mine inspections, the Graff brothers, McNair, and silent partner McKnight incorporated the Royal Mountain Mining Company (Royal Mountain M. Co.) with the Colorado's Secretary of State, on September 15, 1880.

Before the incorporation of this company, the term Royal Mountain or Mount Royal cannot be found in any records referring to this mountain. It is possible that the name of this mountain grew around the first company to own and invest in a majority of it, branding it after the royals they intended to pull from its core.

Ten days after the creation of the Royal Mountain M. Co., the Graff brothers added a new partner to their company, Mr. J.L. Pendery, of Leadville. Pendery served as a lawyer and judge in the Leadville area, along with developments of his own mining ventures.

Before the year 1880 ended, the Royal Mountain M. Co. gained rights to eighteen claims nearing each other on Mount Royal. By March of 1881, the company was in "prosperous condition," with the main tunnel over 100-feet deep, according to the *Leadville Weekly Democrat*. They began using a steam drill and planned to reach a depth of 500-feet come winter. Cross-cutting would then take place to open up several lateral veins.

In May of the same year, Alex Graff purchased 160 acres bound by the Frisco Placer. The main claim of that acreage was a placer founded by his old business partner, the Pendery Placer. Included in the allotted land of this purchase were the mine lodes of the Lebanon, Mamie, Lillie, Gold Anne, and the Victoria.

Following successful mining and developments, the capital stock of the company was placed at $500,000. This total capital was then split into 25,000 shares, each priced at twenty dollars.

By the end of 1881, the Royal Mountain M. Co. held their previous eighteen mining claims, along with an operational stamp mill on their property. This is the first record of a mill within the future Masontown area.

Come 1882, the company was now equipped with an Ingersoll

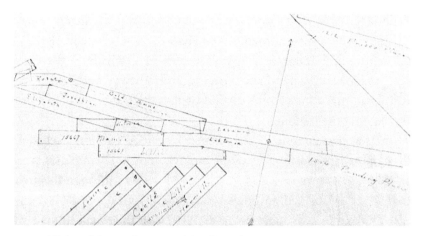

Mining claims under ownership of Royal Mountain Mining Company.
(Frisco Historic Park & Museum)

drill, made by one of mining equipment's leading companies, Ingersoll Rand. This replaced their previous steam drill and assisted them in progressing a consistent forty feet per day into the company's main tunnel.

At the time of his mining the Victoria, Alex Graff proved himself a busy man through his work and community involvement. He was not only heading the Royal Mountain M. Co. along with other business ventures but in addition, was serving as the Mayor of Frisco.

Later in 1882, the Federal Silver Mining Company, not to be confused with Buford's Federal Union Mining Company, filed mining applications for several lodes in this area. A year after the company's incorporation in 1881, they located the Bailey, B.F. Warren, and the Henry D. Foote lodes. These three lodes were situated on the future Masontown property, with the Bailey crossing paths of the Victoria lode. Serving as the company president at this time was J.W. Keifer, and his partners in operations were Henry Foote and Mr. Warren.

In September of 1883, the Federal Silver Mining Company amended its claim to the Bailey, which also included 5.17 acres of land on Mount Royal. This acreage was spanning up the mountain in the opposite direction of Royal Mountain M. Co.'s mill site. The

Federal Silver Mining Company remained active in the area for years to come, with an amendment to the Henry D. Foote lode in 1892.

In the mid-1880s, a man well known in Leadville as the Coal King made his way into Frisco. George H. Hathaway, being this Coal King, had made his empire around fueling the trains that laid track throughout the mountains.

Hathaway, along with his partner, Joseph A. Lamping, set their eyes on expanding their charcoal empire into the Tenmile Canyon as soon as the prominent railroads paved the way through the area. In 1885, they formed an official partnership and opened the kilns just south of Frisco along the DSP&PRR, with their Superintendent of the kilns being John Boyce. While their charcoal operation was bringing in a large sum of money for them, it also required a great amount of timber, resulting in them cutting down an estimated 2,400 acres of forest each year.

The Hathaway-Lamping Kilns outside of Frisco, c.1900
(The John Manley Collection)

Their kilns were constructed in a beehive shape, standing 20-30 feet tall, with a diameter of 40 feet. The process to make their charcoal started with an abundance of timber, which was then slow-cooked in the kilns to create the desired product. As a bushel of charcoal would sell for 30 cents, the laborers who chopped the trees and stoked the ovens could make upwards of six dollars a day.

While the pay that these kilns offered was more desirable than other employment opportunities of the time, it came with its dangers. On March 1, 1887, an employee at the kilns in Frisco suffered a terrible accident while on the clock. As a recently loaded engine powered up to leave the kilns, George Thompson's leg became stuck in the wheels while he dismounted from the train car. He was dragged a reported 50-60 feet, resulting in disfiguration and death. Following the risks of this job, his life policy under the Hathaway-Lamping company was carried out at $6,000.

Succeeding a wood shortage in the 1890s, laws were put in place the limit deforestation, which in turn affected the charcoal industry greatly. Charcoal kilns and their owners now had to make a decision; resort to operating outside the eyes of the law or change their product.

Hathaway and Lamping decided to utilize their previously built kilns in the process of creating coke. Coke was a lightweight fuel that was made by heating coal and removing its impurities. While the railroads still ran on a mixture of timber, coal, and charcoal, their newly produced coke was desirable for running smelters and other mining equipment as it burnt hot and did not deliver much smoke.

The Royal Mountain M. Co. mill was a short-lived venture, as there were no operating stamp mills in Frisco reported through the 1883 *Colorado State Business Directory*. The company, however, appears on state listings for two more years, with no records of its operation after 1885.

Alex Graff remained in town for years to follow. He had left his mining ventures behind him and began a new business as a cattle dealer. Alex, searching for more of a leisure-filled life, was no longer serving as mayor, and was succeeded by Henry Learned. He later moved to Routt County, Colorado, and lived on a ranch just west of the town of Hayden. It was here that he died at the age of 65 in 1894.

Alex was buried in his hometown of Pittsburgh, Pennsylvania.

Unlike his brother, William Graff continued his mining operations after the ending of the Royal Mountain M. Co. He pushed forward on his personal claims to the Caledonia and Mayflower lode, near Mayflower Gulch and Kokomo, which he held since the late 1870s. His work in Frisco continued through his Flora Placer claim, which sat just south of town. William Graff died at the age of 81 on September 6, 1907, after a short illness at his home in Dillon. He too, was buried in Pittsburgh alongside his brother.

No Vacancy

In 1887, a Swedish immigrant named Lars Matsson (sometimes spelt Mattson or Mattsson) arrived countryside. Lars' sister, Carin (Kate) Matsson, had met Frisco's founder Henry Recen in Sweden when he had ventured home in search of his brothers support. Following Henry's tales of riches in the Tenmile Canyon, she was persuaded to join these brothers in America. Kate made her new home in the Recen cabin off the Tenmile Creek and married Henry on July 17, 1876.

Just over ten years after Kate had moved to Frisco, Lars decided to take the voyage in joining his sister. Accompanied by his older brother, Anders (Andrew) Matsson, the party reached Frisco come 1887. Unfortunately, Kate passed away the same year as their arrival.

Despite the death of Lars' sister, the familiar bond remained between him and Henry. Matsson joined the Recen brothers in their mining work, specifically in the Frisco area. The first record of his involvements in Frisco's mining industry was in 1894, where he was listed in the state directory as a mining contractor with partner Recen, and as a mining broker with partner Engstrom. Under their guidance, Matsson began investing in local mining operations and buying property speculated to return good ore.

Four years after his first mention in mining, Matsson continued his work in the industry, this time without Engstrom. He was no longer undertaking contract work, but instead solely held the claim to the lode and its adjoining mines. After his death years later, his obituary, published by the *Summit County Journal*, mentions that Matsson operated "one mine of considerable importance, the Victoria, on Royal Mountain."

Through successful strike after strike, Henry Recen continued to grow his ventures in neighboring Tenmile Canyon towns. As Recens consortium expanded, it also lead to his attention being drawn away from his Frisco claims. When Matsson acquired the Victoria claims, he also began management of Recen's Juno Lode under Excelsior Mine expansion and other claims surrounding Mount Royal. With the placement of these claims alongside the timeline of transfer, it is likely that Matsson gained the Victoria group from the Recens, and possible that the Recens were the first to strike a pick into the ground on this Victoria property nearly twenty years prior.

In 1898, the Denver South Park & Pacific Railroad was purchased and renamed the Colorado & Southern Railroad. This came with the intentions of one large structured company to gain and reorganize several bankrupt or financially unstable railways feeding through Colorado to Denver. For the rest of this book, this line will be referred to as the Colorado & Southern (C&S) in maps and writing.

In November of 1898, three investors secured a lease and bond on the Victoria group from Matsson. Of these men were Messrs. Edwin Hall and Mr. Smith, of nearby Breckenridge, along with Frank Olson, of Kokomo. This trio leased the Victoria and its adjoining claims for the price of $20,000, which was to be paid off to Matsson through monthly payments of one year's time.

The lessees immediately began working a sizable force on the property. Just one month after their purchase, they struck a large body of gold nearing $40-$250 a ton. Excitement ensued, and an increased workforce became necessary to extract the gold.

News of this strike brought miners from all over the state to

Frisco. In fact, the rush of money-hungry miners came in such a volume that the *Summit County Journal* reported all the housing in Frisco had reached capacity. Hall et al were more than satisfied with their purchase, shipping a cart of gold a day as they entered 1899.

Frank Olson and his wife, Atillia, outside of their cabin at Bill's Ranch. (Frisco Historic Park & Museum)

This high-grade ore from the Victoria was being processed at the Smith-Olson Mill, located just north of town and owned by mine lessees Smith and Olson. The high returns of this ore and the efficiency of the mine and mills production attracted famed Breckenridge investor, Capt. Thomas A. Brown, who purchased a one-fourths stake in the mine. Brown had made a career in mining and real estate investments. Still standing in Breckenridge is the Brown Hotel, which Brown purchased and remodeled in the early 1900s.

A meeting within stockholders of the Victoria followed the investment on behalf of Brown. This assembly resulted in Hall as manager of operations and Olson elected as superintendent. Plans for a new reduction plant began thereafter as the gold strike at Victoria continued to mature, reaching a total of 4 feet wide.

Pride and confidence in this local mine soared. It continued to produce wealth for all involved, from miners to investors, bringing with it commerce to local Frisco businesses. The workforce on the Victoria showed no abate as it continued to strike larger bodies than before. On January 14, 1899, the *Summit County Journal* wrote, "No mine in Cripple Creek ever made the showing or shipped the same

John D. Hynderliter, c. 1908
(Frisco Historic Park & Museum)

amount and value of ore, with a like insignificant amount of work done, that the Victoria has."

Following the praise and acclamation of the Victoria, areas surrounding this lode became prized sites to dig. Investors and miners alike held the hopes that their newly discovered lodes would yield the same results seen at their successful neighboring mine. As explorations began to move above the Victoria atop Mount Royal, Hall and Olson opened a new large body of ore nearing their profitable lode.

John D. Hynderliter, a Frisco rancher and once serving Sheriff for the town, also followed suit in exploring the possibilities that sat within this mountain. In April of 1899, he opened a "body of good ore," on his property that sat above the Victoria claim on Mount Royal. He continued to mine these claims for years to come, in hopes of reaching the same riches that Hall et al struck.

In the fall of the same year, Frank T. Botsford, of San Diego, filed suit against the previous Bailey, Warren, and Foote lode owners; the Federal Silver Mining Company. Botsford alleged abandonment on the Mining Application (MA) No. 2330, Bailey lode, which crossed paths of the Victoria. He claimed that this location belonged to him due to abandonment, after Botsford had filed a location to this lode in September of 1898. The hearing was set to take place on September 20, 1899, and was followed with no news of the Bailey lode being granted to Botsford.

While the Foote family name was well known around Summit County, they gained national fame in 1898 after a string of crimes committed by the bandit Pug Ryan.

Robert W. Foote, a cousin of Henry Foote, was the proprietor of the Denver Hotel in Breckenridge, where he saw hundreds of reputable visitors annually. Knowing that the hotel was a constant stream of revenue, a bandit by the name of Arthur Louis Scott, a.k.a. Pug Ryan, set his sights on acquiring Foote's riches.

This photo shows Whitney standing center with a white apron. To his right with the number six under him is Conrad. (Frisco Historic Park & Museum)

Pug was released from Cañon City Prison in May of 1898 and wasted no time before immersing himself in his old ways. Come that August, Pug and his band of outlaws robbed the Denver Hotel at Breckenridge, where they intended to make away with the safe.

Just before midnight on August 11, 1898, Pug, along with Dick

Manley, Fred Wilson, and Dick Bryan, entered the hotel with their revolvers in the air. As they moved towards the safe, one of their guns accidentally fired, resulting in the premeditated plan shifting to a by-the-moment robbery. Pug and his gang began taking money and personal belongings of those in the gambling room and were quickly on their way. The loot stolen contained the Foote family gold watch and a diamond stick pin that Robert Foote was holding for a friend.

Following a $100 reward that Foote put out for the capture of these bandits, recently deputized detective Ernest Conrad accompanied by school board president and saloon owner Sumner Whitney set out for Pug. When they found the gang held out in an abandoned cabin near Kokomo, a gunfight ensued. Conrad was killed instantly, and Whitney was hit by gunfire. Despite his wounds, Whitney was able to fatally strike Manley and kill Bryan. Whitney later died in Leadville from his injury.

Pug managed to evade the law for the next four years, finally being captured in 1902. While awaiting trial in the Leadville Jail, Pug along with five other inmates escaped. He was recaptured shortly after and held for trial in Breckenridge. His claim that they had the wrong person fell to ruins once they rolled up his sleeve, revealing his tattoo reading "PUG". After being found guilty for association to the murder of Conrad, Pug spent the rest of his life in Cañon City Prison. Years later in 1908, two children playing near the fore mentioned cabin in Kokomo discovered a box containing some diamonds, gold chains, revolvers, and Foote's missing watch and stick pen.

As 1899 neared its end, Messrs. Hall, Olson, and Smith failed to make payments on their lease. While the ore's being pulled from the Victoria still held high returns, their ambitions provided their downfall. They continued to invest further throughout the mountain in an attempt to discover new lodes, resulting in their funds being stretched too thin. This failure of lease resulted in their claim to the Victoria group returning into the hands of Matsson.

Dawn of the Century

The new century began and Frisco continued to grow. The first formal Town Hall had just finished construction, and despite its setbacks, managed to open just before the end of the 19th century. Prior to this building, all town matters were discussed in private residents, hotels, or wherever they could find enough seating for officials and townsfolk. Being built off volunteer labor, they had initially hoped for a Fourth of July opening of the building but fell behind schedule. Luckily, they pulled together through the early winter and were able to open for another holiday, Christmas, 1899. They broke-in the building with a grand party, taking sleigh rides to neighboring Dillon, then according to the *Summit County Journal,* they "had a jolly dance until the 'wee small hours." This party, however, was not enough to celebrate the new building as another party took place one week later on New Year's Eve. This old Town Hall now serves as the Visitor Information Center and sits at the corner of Main Street and 3rd Avenue.

Another important building in the history of Frisco was erected this same year, being the Schoolhouse. Oliver Swanson, a local Frisco businessman and owner of the Treasure Vault mine, decided to build a new saloon on the corner of Main Street and Second Avenue in an effort to pull in the business of the town's thirsty mining population. Construction of his saloon was completed in 1899.

While some argue if the saloon ever opened its doors to Frisco's patrons, Swanson is reported to be operating a Main Street saloon according to the 1901 Colorado State Business Directory. November of the same year that he was reported as a saloon owner, Swanson hit financial hardships and sold the building to Simon Schloss of Lake City, Colorado.

Shortly after the purchase on behalf of Schloss, the town of Frisco began looking to construct a new school with hopes that the population would rise following successful mining strikes. After weighing their options, the school board decided to purchase the old Swanson Saloon rather than build a new structure. The cupola and bell found on top of the building were next purchased from an 1882 Breckenridge schoolhouse. This final adjustment completed the new education building, and class in the Frisco Schoolhouse was in session.

After over 50 years of hosting the children of Frisco, the last class was held here in 1963. Since then this building served as the School Board offices, and in 1983, began its new life as the museum it still is today. While visiting the museum you can still see signs of the building's past lives. A cut out hatch remains on the hardwood floor, leading down to the old cellar and water well for Swanson's Saloon. The attic on top of the Schoolhouse, which now serves as museum storage, was once the dwelling space for teachers of Frisco.

Frisco's population remained in the 200s as they entered the 20th Century, and mining investors watched closely, awaiting a new mining strike to draw in the fortune they desired.

At this time, the Victoria group was only partially leased. Miners E.W. Hallen and Mr. Kogsberg leased and worked a portion of these claims on behalf of Matsson, while Matsson and his new partner, Mr. Westland, developed the rest of the claims. Their focus at this time was crosscutting the lower veins rather than reaching new depths in the Victoria's main tunnel.

The Frisco Schoolhouse, c.1910 (Frisco Historic Park & Museum)

Mining developments continued throughout the year, and Matsson neared completion on a sale of the Victoria group to an eastern syndicate. Mr. Person, of St. Louis, who held the intentions of putting up an amalgamating and concentrating plant on the property, headed the interested company. Luckily for Person, Matsson had an area already proven successful for milling. This proposed plot contained stream access and graded flat grounds nearing the mine entrances, the old Royal Mountain M. Co. Mill site.

Included in this sale to Mr. Person were six adjoining mining claims, owned by Frisco's mayor at the time, Harry Britton. It was through this sale that the size and reach of the future Masontown property began to magnify. It grew past the concentrated Victoria group of claims, spanning into the entirety of the property we recognize today.

After the loss of the prior year's lawsuit, Frank T. Botsford attempted once again to stake his claim within the Victoria group of mines. While he had no success in claiming abandonment of specific lodes, he did gain partial control over the surrounding mines through deed. On February 24, 1900, Frank and Victoria Judson deeded all of their interests in the Stonewall, Frank, Pretty Slick, Botsford, Terrell, and Victoria lodes, along with interest in the Victoria Mill site, to Botsford. Shortly after, John B. Killgore transferred his interests of the Foote, B.F. Warren, and Bailey lodes to Botsford on May 5. This did not make Botsford the owner of claims that he had initially desired but gave him a stake in the future profits of this area.

Former Victoria lessee Frank Olson reentered his work with the Victoria group in 1902. He had recently relocated himself and his family to Frisco from neighboring Kokomo the year before and looked to pick back up where he left his mining ventures three years prior. Once in town, Olson and partner Frank B. Wiborg, of Cincinnati, patented 1,500 linear feet of the Mamie and Lillie lodes. These two lodes were adjoined to the claims of Victoria and Lebatoria lodes.

The Admiral Gold Mining Company, which had recently been incorporated by Abel H. Frost and E.E. Busby, also joined involvement in the claims of this area. On August 23, 1902, Frank T. Botsford sold all of his interests in the B.F. Warren and Henry D. Foote lodes to Frost. At that same time, Abel H. Frost transferred his personal claims of the Frank and Botsford lodes to his newly formed company. As the Admiral Gold Mining Company progressed and stabilized its founding, Frost continued the transference of his personal deeds and interest near the Victoria to the company.

Near the end of 1902, another failure to pay on this property's lease occurred. This time on behalf of lessee Mr. Person, whose eastern-based company did not receive the timely payout that they desired.

Person forfeited his claim back into the hands of Matsson, who resumed his personal work further into the Victoria. Matsson reduced his workforce and once again shifted operations to explore across the veins rather than obtaining new depths. The Victoria continued as a regular shipper of high-grade ore, and Matsson began looking into the possibility of a lower adit.

Word of a new sale on the property began floating around town, though it was not finalized until the following year.

For What it is Named

In October of 1903, a man by the name of Albert Elisha Keables traveled to Frisco from Denver. Born in Iowa in 1859, Keables had relocated to Colorado with his family at the age of ten and attended school in Colorado City. Years later, he brought with him to Frisco the aims of managing mining operations, along with a specific interest in the Victoria. Keables' partner, an expert mill man, traveled from Masontown, Pennsylvania, with confidence to develop successful mines just as he had done back home.

Upon a possible property sale, Matsson began making improvements to his old mill site. He purchased materials from the Wilson smelter that sat outside of town, bringing them to his property to improve Victoria's ore processing. About forty-five loads of lumber and machinery were hauled to the Victoria Mill site by way of the wagon. Heading this transportation was William H. Staley, a Frisco resident, and freighter. Staley would later reach his demise in an intoxicated freighting accident returning to Frisco from Breckenridge on October 17, 1908.

In September of 1903, the Masontown Mining and Milling Company (Masontown M. & M. Co.) was organized and incorporated with the primary purpose of operating this mine. The name Masontown was chosen to reflect the hometown of company president, J.V. Hoover, who built his business mining in Masontown, Pennsylvania. After incorporation by the state, Masontown M. & M. Co. was capitalized at $1,500,000, which would be just short of $45 million today. Serving alongside company president Hoover was Silas R. Provins, of Greensboro, PA, acting as treasurer, and Keables acting as secretary.

William Staley and his family. (Frisco Historic Park & Museum)

Immediately after their incorporation, the company purchased the Victoria group and property from Matsson. Instantaneous plans were underway to place a stamp mill with an attached cyanide plant on the old mill site. This was their top priority since the mill's installment would result in cutting costs of processing and shipping the ore.

Instead of building a new mill from the ground up or converting the old Victoria Mill, the company purchased the Smith-Olson stamp mill. This same mill was the one used to process the gold from the 1898 Victoria strike and was owned by previous Victoria lessees Frank Olson and Mr. Smith. The mill was to be taken apart, transported to its new location, and then reassembled in a modified fashion at the site of the old Victoria Mill. George Wortman, an acclaimed engineer with several patents working for the Climax Mine just north of Leadville, headed the transportation and construction for this project. Hoover's plans for the new mill determined its size to be 50 by 140 feet, complete with 20 stamps and several cyanide attachments.

While mill construction was underway, Masontown M. & M. Co. mined the Victoria at great force. They were working all available men and held the mindset that nothing could stop their imminent success.

On March 22, 1904, Lars Matsson died at his home in Frisco after a short struggle with pneumonia. In the *Summit County Journal's* posting of his death, it shares that Matsson sold his property of the Victoria group to Masontown M. & M. Co. for $25,000. This recent sale was $5,000 more than his previous lease of 1898 to Messrs. Hall, Smith, and Olson.

Construction of the new mill continued through the death of Matsson, and the Masontown Mill opened on June 1, 1904. The plant was electrically lit and ran with the "accuracy of a watch," reported the *Summit County Journal* under their "Mining News" section.

This new mill was equipped with the best technologies available at the time and was acclaimed to be an immaculate producer. Its process began with ore moved up a tramway entrance and dumped to a platform near the top of the mill. The ore then passed through a Blake crusher into a bin sized for sixty to seventy tons. After exiting through the bin gates, the ore then went through automatic feeders into four battery boxes, which contained twenty stamps. The crushed pulp from these stamps flowed down to concentrating tables, where the minerals would be extracted and the remainder would run off into cyanide tanks. The method that this mill had put in place maximized the output of gold, as both the cyanide precipitates and the gold amalgam could be processed into gold bars. The cost of both the mining and milling process fell just short of $2 a ton.

Succeeding the successful opening of the new stamp mill, an election was held among stockholders of the Masontown M. & M. Co. Hoover and Provins remained in their positions as president and treasurer, while Keables was promoted to superintendent and manager of mines. New partners and elects in the company included David H. Lawrence, of Breckenridge, who was elected as superintendent of milling operations, and Frank Graham, of Summit County, who was elected as company assayer. The company stock remained at a total of $1,500,000; however, their property now included twelve load claims, a mill, one placer claim, and covered roughly 100 acres of land.

Keables and Lawrence were no strangers and had been working together in the mining industry years prior. Lawrence was born in Adelaide, Australia, where he graduated from the University of Adelaide's School of Mines with a Bachelor of Science. He then traveled to major mining countries around the world, eventually landing in Summit County, Colorado. Upon his arrival, he quickly paired with Keables, sitting as Consulting and Reporting Engineer for the Summit County Mining Exchange, a highly regarded company that Keables started in Breckenridge. They also shared managerial positions at the Washington Mining & Milling Company and the Union Mining & Milling Company. To further the bond between these two, they were both fraternal members of the Breckenridge Lodge of Masons and the Loyal League.

While some took to Leadville or Dillon for the 1904 Fourth of July, dozens attended the celebrations held at Masontown. Hoover organized wagon rides from Frisco to his bustling mine, including a stop at nearby Uneva Lake. Upon arrival, the attendants took part in hiking, wildflower picking, fishing, and a picnic. Food was cooked and served by George Wortman and his wife Lillie. After George conducted his work on the Masontown Mill construction, he and his wife operated the boarding house on the company's property. The *Breckenridge Bulletin* wrote that "All declared themselves delighted with the days outing in the lovely spot selected."

Masontown M. & M. Co. finished out the year 1904 with a strike of 20-30 feet of good ore. This strike was a new length record for the Victoria group property.

An unknown man standing above Masontown Mill. The tramway where ore entered the mill can be seen from this angle. (Frisco Historic Park & Museum.)

This exterior view shows the power lines that electrically lit the mine, mill, offices, quarters, and rest of camp. (Mining Reporter, Volume 51, 1905)

An interior view of the Masontown Mill and amalgamating plates, c. 1905.
(Mining Reporter, Volume 51, 1905)

The solution tanks and precipitation boxes of the Masontown Mill, c. 1905.
(Mining Reporter, Volume 51, 1905)

Evelina Hedenskog Pridy stands outside of a mine entrance at Masontown.
(Frisco Historic Park & Museum)

Issues over ownership of the company presented themselves in 1905, causing a shutdown of operations for most of the year. Disputes over lawful transfer began after the death of Matsson, and upon reaching the public eye, resulted in lawsuits between the company founders. The original property lease and bond from Matsson were given to Provins and Hoover personally, along with a deed in escrow. This was all to be transferred to the Masontown M. & M. Co. after the finalization of the sale. These errors in the transfer were noticed after the construction of the new mill and other improvements to the mine overall, resulting in an increase in property value. Provins, after reevaluating what his deed would now be worth, refused the transfer of his temporary ownership to the company as agreed upon.

In August, after several trips around the country on behalf of Hoover, the company filed suit for liberation. Hoover gained the support and trust of Frisco locals and mine employees throughout these affairs, as they believed he had the best interests of the workers in mind. In an effort to keep employees working throughout the lawsuits and shutdown, Hoover had improvements done to the mill. This was done so that when the time came to resume operations, they would be ready to mine and mill at full capacity.

Luckily, it was not long before these affairs were settled and full-scale work on the property resumed in early October of 1905. By the end of the month, the lease and bond rested rightfully in the hands of the Masontown M. & M. Co. and its stockholders.

Keables and Lawrence, eager to make up for lost time, began more aggressive work on their mine. They sunk their main shaft to cut sulfide ore and installed a hoisting plant on the property. At this time Lawrence was also the lead engineer for the claims near Uneva Lake on behalf of the North American Mining Company.

Before the end of 1905, the Admiral Gold Mining Company amended their location and partial ownership to the claims of the Pretty Slick and Victoria lode, along with the Victoria Mill site.

Daniel Recen (Frisco Historic Park & Museum)

More lawsuits plagued the company in 1906, stemming from the passing and deed of Lars Matsson. Daniel Recen, the former partner of Matsson and brother of Frisco's founder Henry Recen, sued the estate for a $2,500 commission of the $25,000 sale to Masontown M. & M. Co. that took place in 1903. His basis was that of an oral agreement between Matsson and himself, which would grant him ten percent commission if the property were to ever sell instead of lease. The sale in suit was to the claim of the Victoria, Lebanon, and Gold Anne lodes, and the mill site. This lawsuit was unsuccessful on Recen's end, as there was no tangible evidence of said oral agreement.

The Masontown M. & M. Co., becoming more accustomed to lawsuits, wasted no time resuming operations. They shipped out loads returning up to $90 a ton the following month.

In October of 1906, another Pennsylvania mining associate took a trip to Masontown to see after the Victoria mine. George W. Hibbs traveled from Fayette, Pennsylvania, to meet with Hoover and Keables for a supposed tour and consultation of the mining and milling operations. While it was not clear what his intentions were to the workers, the sense of him sticking around for the future seemed to be absolute.

Around the same time as the visit from Hibbs, a new member was added to the team, being John Percy Hart. A tall, slim man, Hart was noted for always paying attention to his appearance. Whether he was sitting in on a shareholder's meeting or touring his dark and dusty mines, his three-piece suit is remembered to always have been in attendance. Like many of the property's previous owners and managers, Hart did not veer from par, being from Pennsylvania.

The company elected Hart as manager of operations. Before his new title, Hart had been a prominent stockholder in the Masontown M. & M. Co. since 1904. He, along with his wife Finley and their three

children, Dale, Melissa, and John Percy Jr., moved into a cabin on the Masontown property. His first task as manager was to improve the mill by replacing cyaniding with agitation.

In December of 1906, George B. Raynor, on behalf of the Admiral Gold Mining Company, renewed the partial patent on the Bailey, Victoria, and Pretty Slick lodes, along with the Victoria Mill site. The company also purchased the Terrill, Admiral, and Chicago lodes, which sat just below the Victoria.

John Percy Hart, c. 1911
(Frisco Historic Park & Museum)

In With the New

On October 31, 1906, after a promising tour of the Victoria, George W. Hibbs incorporated the Hibbs Mining and Milling Company (Hibbs M. & M. Co.). By that November, the Masontown M. & M. Co. had abruptly ended its operations leaving the mine's employees rolling over to the new ownership, being Hibbs. This included their mill site, mining claims, and acreage. A 1907 map of property and claims owned by Hibbs M. & M. Co. surveyed by L.A. Wildhack shows the following mining claims:

> *Victoria, Lebanon, Lebatoria, Gold Anne, Josephine, Elizabeth, Rosie, Harietta, Lillian, Cecile, Louisa No. 1, Louisa No. 2, Louisa No. 3, Leona Placer,* and the *Victoria Mill site.*

Despite the change in ownership, J. Percy Hart remained the manager and head of operations through the company transfer. For Hart, everything was business as usual when it came to his operations. No matter who owned the claims, Hart intended to maximize profits for the sake of all involved. He worked three shifts of men and reached the company's first sizable strike of the year in February. Alongside Hart from the previous Masontown M. & M. Co. stood David H. Lawrence, now serving as the company's engineer.

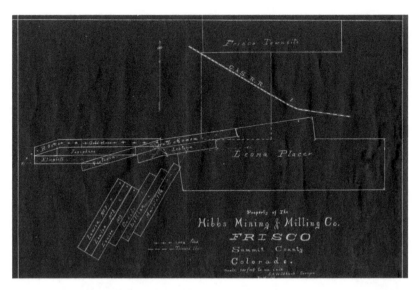

August 17, 1907 map, surveyed by L.A. Wildhack. This map shows Hibbs Mining and Milling Company mining claims, along with the Colorado & Southern Railroad and Frisco town site. (Frisco Historic Park & Museum)

The first large-scale alteration to the property under Hibbs M. & M. Co. happened in June. Their plans were to undercut the Victoria vein by an estimated 500 feet. This would allow transportation of ore to come out of an adit at an elevation level with the Colorado & Southern railroad tracks rather than shipping it the mile down the mountain. This lower section would also serve the purpose of unwatering the mountain.

In addition to a lower adit, the company proposed to move the cyanide mill to that same level. Once relocation of the mill took place, they would then add more concentrating tables for treatment of custom ores. The ambitions of this new company exceeded their actions, as the mill was never relocated to this area.

In April of 1907, the Admiral Gold Mining Company closed its connections to the Masontown property. They did so by relinquishing their holdings on the Admiral and Victoria to the Aztec Mines Company for $1.00.

Aligning with his career in local mines and his dedication to seeing those around him acknowledged for their efforts, Hart started up his own monthly publication. Prior to moving to Frisco, Hart had worked as a compositor for a printing company. Having this know-how and skill set, he took on the writing and publishing by himself. In late 1907, the *Successful Miner* went into circulation, highlighting the mines of the Tenmile Canyon and its neighboring districts. However, publishing his own paper proved to be financially draining as Hart reached out for sponsorship to help with his printing costs early the following year. This newspaper, while loved by local miners, never gained the widespread acclaim he had hoped, leading to its discontinuation.

In 1907, operating Victoria engineer David H. Lawrence along with previous property manager Albert E. Keables found themselves at the wrong end of the law in what would become one of the most famed wildcat mine schemes of this time. As they continued to share employers and mining ventures with numerous mining companies, their luck on turning profits together hit a turn under the leadership of George S. DuBois, of Boulder, Colorado.

George S. DuBois, accompanied by his son Lee, formed the Lost Bullion Spanish Mine Company out of New Mexico, mid-1906. The first strike of this company came on December 26 of that year and resulted in rediscovering a sunken mine from 1875, still bearing its riches. As previously proven by those seeking lost treasure, many jumped at the chance to be involved with this forgotten trove.

Upon further chasing the theme of lost mines and their associated investors, Mr. DuBois next claimed that an old Native American visited their mine office with information that would further the company. This man told them of a lost Spanish mine from the 16th century that was worked with Native slave labor. Upon a slave insurrection, the Spaniards were forced to abandon the mine, leaving behind all the gold that lay within. The DuBois began to explore the nearby property on Bear Mountain, just outside of Silver City, New Mexico, and came across the fore mentioned mine.

Two weeks after rediscovering this mine, DuBois hired William

H. Wilson as president of the company, assured that he would secure the proper investments to excavate the area. Wilson then brought in two engineers, one of them being Lawrence, to determine the remaining ore value.

To attract investors, brochures titled *A Glimpse into the Mysteries and Secrets of the Treasure Vaults of the Ancient Spaniards* were mailed around the country projecting that the already exposed veins would yield $31 million, based off the three assays that had been done. The company headquarters was then moved to Denver, where Keables was added to the managerial roster.

Just three months after the discovery of the Spanish mines, warrants were issued for those involved with the company. After an outside source evaluation was done, it showed that the "mine" was nothing more than a limestone cave. Thanks to their bountiful self-evaluation in the sent brochures, an estimated $30,000 were invested into the company through fraudulent claims of gold. While some company executives fled the state, eleven arrests were made. Both Lawrence and Keables were of these eleven, along with their business partner from the Summit County Mining Exchange, Carle Lamont Blackman, of Breckenridge. Before joining the Summit County Mining Exchange in 1905, Blackman looked over treasury interests of the Masontown M. & M. Co. as a contractor for Keables.

As it would turn out, the mailing of these brochures proved their downfall in the case brought on by postal authorities Charles Riddiford and C.A. Macomie. On April 6, 1907, the men arrested went on trial, officially charged with "mailing letters in pursuance of scheme to defraud." The case was held in the United States District Court for the District of Colorado under future United States federal judge, Robert E. Lewis.

Both Keables and Lawrence were sentenced on August 25, 1907, to serve fifteen days in jail along with a $500 fine on the charges of conspiracy and the fraudulent use of mail. Blackman and DuBois received the heavier sentence, being thirty days in jail and $1,000 fine. The company attempted several appeals, yet it was not until the final ruling in December of 1911 that those sentenced had to pay their dues. DuBois, however, never had to carry out his sentence as he was shot and killed in Balarat, Colorado, just outside of Boulder in early April of 1908. The quarrel that ended his life was one over an outstanding boarding house bill.

David H. Lawrence left his work in Frisco and the Masontown property shortly after this scandal. He continued to consult as a mining engineer in Denver until his death in 1920.

By 1919, Keables had relocated to San Francisco, where he would continue in the mining industry. Speculations around trusting him only worsened after the Lost Bullion case, which was later supported by several other small-scale mining fraud charges in Sacramento, California. Keables remained in Sacramento until his death on February 8, 1927. Following his fraternal memberships, Keables is buried in the Masonic Lawn Cemetery in Sacramento, California.

As the year of 1908 arrived, so did news of the death of J.V.

George B. Robinson
(Frisco Historic Park & Museum)

Hoover, of the Masontown M. & M. Co. He died in early January, in his home town of Masontown, Pennsylvania. While Hoover was no longer involved with the Victoria mine, the Frisco townsfolk remembered him fondly as a man who fought for the rights of the miners, always holding the interests of his employees at the forefront of his actions.

The following April, Hart took a trip to Pennsylvania to have a meeting with eastern stockholders of the company. This meeting was held in the hopes of raising funds for mill improvements, including the installation of a new oxidizing method to replace the current cyaniding. His partner in this funding presentation was the president of Hibbs M. & M. Co., Dr. A.W. Clark, of Omaha, Nebraska.

Mill fundraising was not successful, and financial troubles struck the company in October of 1909. This is demonstrated in a letter from Hart to George B. Robinson, who was then serving as County Treasurer. Hart asked Robinson not to publish the delinquent taxes on the property in the upcoming newspaper and stated that he would return to town with the first payment after his most recent trip concluded. The request was granted, and there was no mention of Hibbs M. & M. Co. or the Masontown property in the following issue's list of delinquent mine taxes.

Hart, always being the overachiever that had progressed him throughout his life, decided to continue his community-focused role for the town he was so proud to be operating within. In 1909, he was re-elected for a second term as mayor of Frisco, all while remaining manager of the Hibbs M. & M. Co.

Property and buildings of the Hibbs Mining and Milling Company.
(Frisco Historic Park & Museum)

The company held new managerial elections in late 1909. They resulted in Hart now taking on the additional roles of treasurer and secretary, along with his previous title of general manager and Frisco's Mayor. Operating under his new handful of roles, Hart continued progress on the mine, drilling deeper in an effort to reach their goals of an ore shoot level with the railroad.

Dr. A.W. Clark, still serving as company president, along with investors Rev. Warren P. Clark and R.E. Stewart, visited town in June of 1910 to see after their investments. They were pleased to report Hart's successful work, along with the mines new 65-foot winze. This winze connected two levels and crossed the character of ore, changing from an oxide to a heavy iron sulfide, which was more likely to carry gold and silver. The driving of the lower tunnel was also in great condition, much to the pleasure of Clark and other investors. The company held plans to open the ore chute level with the railroad before the end of summer.

After three years of mining the area following their purchase from the Admiral Gold Mining Company, the dissolution of the Aztec Mines Company took place on December 17, 1910. In those years, the company had opened six lodes, named the Aztec and the Aztec No. 1-5.

The last report of workings on behalf of the Hibbs M. & M. Co. came in the April edition of the *School of Mines Quarterly*, 1911. This publication commended the company for successfully driving a 100-foot crosscut, and listed a workforce of twenty men. They also reported that the company's cyanide treatment was not giving the best results and that they had plans to rebuild the mill with modern technologies.

By 1915, the *Engineering and Mining Journal* listed the Hibbs M. & M. Co. among other defunct Colorado mining companies.

An Effectual Remedy

A new company headed by Hart was formed at the tail end of 1910. Under the name Frisco Mining, Milling, and Development Company (Frisco M. M. & D. Co.), their plans were to resume where Hibbs M. & M. Co. left off on Mount Royal, along with incorporating more claims and new tunnel routes to the property.

Hart's first actions under this new company came as a publication in 1911. The Frisco M. M. & D. Co. published a 32-page pamphlet, called *An Effectual Remedy for the Evils in Mining and Mining Companies.* This pamphlet's purpose was to inform possible investors of the company's intentions and their plans for mining into Mount Royal.

The company had recently acquired the John D. Hynderliter claims, above the Victoria, and intended to explore the tunnels in a route previously untouched. They also mentioned that they were in the process of locating thirty more claims nearing those of Hynderliter and surrounding the Victoria.

Their planned ore shoot crossed the path of the main tunnel of the King Solomon Tunnel & Development Company, another major company mining on the opposite side of Mount Royal. Hart proposed the idea of the two entities working together to share this shoot and received a positive response from Sam H. Alexander, vice president of the King Solomon Co. Alexander wrote a letter encouraging this proposal and assuring the success of Hart based on his previous actions, which was included in Hart's publication.

On the last page of this pamphlet, Hart attached a credit certificate to be filled out and mailed back by anyone interested in purchasing stock with the company. Stocks were priced at 12.5 cents each, in a groping of 1,000 shares for $25.

CREDIT CERTIFICATE

GOOD FOR $25.00

This certificate will be accepted as part payment for the purchase of 1,000 shares of the capital stock of THE FRISCO MINING, MILLING AND DEVELOPMENT COMPANY at 12½ cents per share, providing the subscriber is the owner of shares in some other mining company.

I own ....shares of stock of the ....

....Company.

NAME.. POSTOFFICE..............................

CITY (OR TOWN) .... STATE ....

SEE PAGE 32 FOR SUBSCRIPTION BLANK TO BE USED IN CONJUNCTION WITH THIS CERTIFICATE

Credit Certificate included in Hart's pamphlet.
(Frisco Historic Park & Museum)

At the time of this publication, Hart was serving as secretary, manager, and treasurer of the Frisco M. M. & D. Co. Alongside him serving as company president was John W. Lynn, of Omaha, Nebraska.

In May of 1911, consolidation of the Victoria group and its neighboring mines took place, and the old Victoria site and its claims were relocated. By January of 1912, the Frisco M. M. & D. Co. was operating this property along with their Hynderliter claims. Hart remained in his position of manager, along with newly elected Frank Cherryholmes, former Frisco Marshall and Sheriff, as superintendent. They were working a force of four men to move past a long cave-in of the Lebanon lode, with plans of increasing the work force soon after the cleanup.

Frank Cherryholmes holding his catch of the day. (Frisco Historic Park & Museum)

The following July, Frederick William Echternkamp was hired onto the Frisco M. M. & D. Co. He was placed in charge of getting the property back in working order and pushing the tunnels deeper to reach ore in their lower levels.

Echternkamp, previously a farmer in Miller Township, Knox County, Nebraska, sold off his property and moved to Frisco to begin

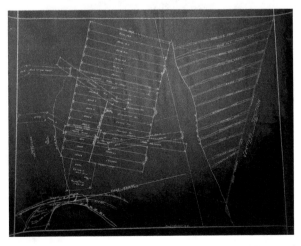

Map of the 1911 consolidated claims. (Frisco Historic Park & Museum)

his role for the Frisco M. M. & D. Co. Accompanying him on this new venture was his wife Elizabeth, and their three youngest children, Bryan, Stevenson, and Goldie.

John W. Lynn, President of Frisco Mining Milling and Development Company, c. 1911. (Frisco Historic Park & Museum)

Back to Basics

The intended plans of the Frisco M. M. & D. Co. did not reach their goal, resulting in a loss to their claims. By 1913, just three years after their founding, the company dissolved and left its plans of pursuing the riches within Mount Royal behind.

J. Percy Hart, after several attempts to turn the Masontown property into a successful venture, retired from mining this area. By 1920, he and his family had relocated to Los Angeles, California. Here, he continued in his underground excavation, only this time to be working on the sewer system of the city. Later in his life, he switched careers to a sales position at an auto store. Hart passed away on February 27, 1947, in his home on 57th Avenue, Los Angeles, California.

On Saturday, April 5, 1913, all mining claims, equipment, and buildings of the old Hibbs Mining & Milling Company, most recently owned by the Frisco M. M. & D. Co., went on auction to the highest bidder.

Echternkamp, after being recently hired on by the Frisco M. M. & D. Co., had a chance to explore the tunnels, veins, and possibilities throughout the property before their closure. Being familiar with this plot and its potential, Echternkamp placed a bid in the auction. With no others jumping at the bit to secure this land, he won the auction and acquired the claim to the Victoria mine and its mill. Instead of pursuing with a large workforce like the many owners before him, Echternkamp held the intention of developing the property on his own.

Echternkamp spent much of 1914 bringing the mineshafts and machinery back into working order. The rest of his year was busy with lawsuits filed against Echternkamp by the Frisco M. M. & D. Co. along with rowdy children smashing the windows and stealing the door to the Hibbs Mill on his property.

By 1915, Echternkamp finally reached the vein that he wanted with the help of his two sons, Bryan and Stevenson. He hit bedrock and was "sure to be in the ore soon," according to the *Summit County Journal*. The following year, he and his family were still mining the vein, with reports of his property housing "a large plant and machinery, including a mill."

Unfortunately, after five years of mining the area, Echternkamp could not pull out the ore he had desired with his purchase of these claims. After giving it his best, accompanied by the work and help of his family, they called it quits on the Victoria in 1918. He, his wife, and his children packed up and moved from Frisco to Craig, Colorado. It was here that he had purchased a ranch that they intended on living at full time, leaving his mining work behind him in Frisco. In 1922, after just four years of ranching his property, Frederick passed away at the age of 65.

Sliding Down the Mountain

In the spring of 1926, a snow slide came rushing down Victoria Mountain, burying the C&S railroad tracks beneath in forty feet of snow. The line of this slide, which can be seen today scarring the side of Victoria Mountain, was right on track to hit the campsite of old Masontown. It destroyed all of what remained standing on this once heavily worked camp, sparing just one cabin.

Harold "Chick" Demming, an early Frisco local, reminisced on this slide through a letter addressing his upbringing in Frisco. His letter recalls memories of this slide, along with snowshoeing to the ruins with the other Demming brothers to camp in the remaining cabin.

Demming also mentions another slide that debilitated the property years before this. He wrote that the 1926 slide was the second destructive one there, with the first being around 1912.

The story of the original demise of Masontown happened on New Year's Eve, 1911. It is said that the camp's miners and workers all traveled to Frisco for the night to celebrate, leaving their camp empty. Amongst the festivities, they heard a loud roar growing in the distance. Tracks showed an avalanche had struck the property, and miners rushed up Mount Royal, only to find their camp in ruins.

While there is no documentation of this slide occurring on New

Year's Eve, it very well could have been the one leading to the Lebanon lode cave-in and clean-up that took place in late January of 1912. This was reported in the local papers, and cleaned by Hart in order to resume operations. It is also at this time that Echternkamp was hired by Frisco M. M. & D. Co. to come and bring the property back into working order. The timing of the two incidents aligns correctly and could have possibly been the New Year's Eve slide that locals recall.

Another Frisco local, Helen Rich, was quoted saying, "Slides come down regularly in the Masontown area. Nobody bothers to keep tabs on them, and apparently didn't in the earlier days, either."

Slides are no stranger to this area, and have presented issues throughout the years spent mining here. In 1899, Jack Spratt, a Summit County resident, not to be confused with the man from the nursery rhyme, reported a slide hitting the mouth of the Victoria Tunnel. This slide covered the mine entrance and destroyed the wagon road to the railway from the camp. Olson, the lessee of the property at the time, reported that the storm did not slow operations. Workers spent some time clearing the road resulting in shipments being slightly delayed, but were back to regular shipments within weeks.

Another possibility of the devastating New Year's Eve slide told in 1911 could once again be the blending of stories. The Hibbs M. & M. Co. ceased operations in 1911, leaving major workings at the mill bare. Near this same time, the slide that caved in a mine nearing the Victoria took place. This shutdown of the Hibbs Mill, paired with the slide caving in the Lebanon lode of January 1912, along with the slide leading to mill decimation in 1926, could have combined over time into one story of an avalanche that destroyed the mill and property on New Years of 1911.

It is likely that if the New Year's slide of 1911 did strike the Masontown property, it did not render the mill and mine useless, as we see accounts of the mill past this date. Such accounts are the Hibbs Mill going to auction in 1913, Echternkamp reporting vandalism to his mill windows and machinery in 1914, and an account of the old Hibbs mill being on the Echternkamp property in 1916.

Photo taken of Masontown property after the 1926 slide.
(Frisco Historic Park & Museum)

From the Rubble

After the slide of 1926, not much was left on the Masontown property other than the sole cabin, scattered rubble, and a few mineshafts. Locals still frequented this area, taking hiking trips to the ruins and exploring what remained. It is told that one snowy night a hiker came rushing down Mount Royal to the Bill's Ranch property, south of Frisco proper, yelling for the help of his wife who went into labor at the ghost town. Jane Thomas, beloved woman of early Frisco, rushed with this man up the mountain and delivered a healthy set of twins in the midst of a blizzard. Acts like this were not unusual for Mrs. Thomas, as locals referred to her as a "pint-sized powerhouse" who was known for breaking up barroom brawls despite her standing less than five feet tall.

Mining operations continued around the Masontown property after the slide, but never fully for the exploration of the Victoria mine. The Frisco Tunnel and King Solomon Company remained operating on Mount Royal several years after Echternkamp ceased his mining, with the Frisco Tunnel being mined into the 1930s.

It is said that a man referred to as "Mr. Morrison" mined the Masontown property in the 1930s, investing $50,000 with no return. It is possible that he attempted to revive this once busy camp, yet no records of him can be found. This lack of information, however, is not surprising for this time, as the population of Frisco dropped down to 18 residents in 1930.

Local legend tells of a new type of workforce occupying this camp throughout the 1920s. Prohibition of alcohol in Colorado lasted from 1916 to 1933, which preceded the beginning of the 18th Amendment by four years. As state officials began to bust saloons that still sold alcohol, the proprietors of these watering holes began to hide their actions. Older bars that are still operating in Summit County tell of their secret back rooms during this time, serving as a safe haven for local patrons to avoid these new laws.

A copper whiskey still, similar to what would have been used at this time to make moonshine. (Frisco Historic Park & Museum)

Importing alcohol from neighboring states carried an increased hassle after the countrywide ban, leading to more moonshiners operating within Colorado. Newspapers began reporting on large distillery busts in the mountains outside of Glenwood Springs,

Denver, and other major cities in the state. While the smaller mountain communities did not receive the same public attention, they were certainly hosting the same operations. Frisco tales tell of moonshiners occupying the Masontown property in the 1920s with whiskey stills hidden in old structures and mine entrances. If one was looking to hide operations from the public, what better place to do so than a ghost town halfway up Mount Royal?

There are no official records of any moonshining busts taking place at this location, but that does not mean that it never happened. After all, the basis of moonshining was to be discreet and avoid being caught.

The structures of old Masontown remained in ruins where they originally sat until the 1960s. In 1968, the Forest Service declared that they posed a forest fire risk to the area and plans began to remove the materials. They had the remaining rubble destroyed in a controlled burn that year. What currently sits in this area are a few tailing piles, brick foundations, some metal artifacts, and a lower adit.

The remains of Masontown prior to the controlled burn, c. 1968.
(Frisco Historic Park & Museum)

Richard Sullivan and his wife Sondra at the remaining Masontown cabin before his deployment to Europe, c. 1957. (Personal Collection of Dick Sullivan)

The Hedenskog children and friends standing on a boiler at the Masontown ruins, c.1932. (Frisco Historic Park & Museum)

Conclusion

Throughout numerous owners, leasers and lessees, individuals, and companies, the Victoria mine played a large role in the history of Frisco. The excitement and action of strikes in this mine brought investors from all over the country to Frisco and had them returning home with nothing but praises for the growing town. Many of Frisco's early residents moved to the area and were employed through the development and operations of this mine. Mayors of the town were brought to the county and fell in love with the area through this mine. Former Frisco Mayor and Victoria manager J. Percy Hart, originally from Pennsylvania, was quoted after a business trip to Nebraska saying that he "would rather be the flag pole on Peak One than the mayor of Omaha."

While miners and industry workers alike came here in search of wealth, that was never quite their result. One reoccurring theme that led to the demise of several companies on this property was that their ambitions exceeded the magnitude of nearby minerals. They would have a successful strike in one tunnel, then immediately begin digging new exploratory winzes, returning no pay ore in the process. Another outlier for this mine is that all of its operators continued in pursuit of gold, whereas most mines of Frisco found their luck in silver. All the presented issues paired with the privations of unpredictable winters, alongside a mile haul to the nearest railroad or town, this camp held spirits higher than their ore returns.

Despite previous failures, the attraction to Mount Royal and its possible riches remained prominent as the years moved past. Whether the Masontown property was nothing more than an outpost, a small mining camp, or a populated company town in itself, it is certain that the Victoria mines' presence in the area and the business that it created held instrumental in the support and development of the new and growing town of Frisco.

The Hiking Guide

Hiking Guide

Masontown, along with the Mount Royal Trail, is owned and maintained by the Colorado Forest Service. While on this trail, it is of utmost importance to respect the environment that surrounds the old town. Due to its fragile ecosystem, protected wildlife and plant life, and cultural/historical significance, items must be left as they are found and all Forest Service signage must be followed.

A map of the described hike is located on page 79.
Hiking Guide illustrations by Amber Zundel.

To begin your hike to Masontown, start by parking in the large lot off Exit 201 for Frisco, at the intersection of Main Street and I-70 at coordinates 39°34'30.4"N 106°06'39.9"W. Before leaving your car, take into account that the hike to Masontown is just short of one mile with an elevation gain of 500 feet (one way). If you wish to continue to the peak of Mount Royal after the trail it will be just under two miles with an elevation gain of 1,400 feet (one way). Consider how much water and what supplies will be necessary for you and your party, then adjust or continue accordingly.

From the parking lot, begin along the Recreation Path and you will cross the wooden bridge over the Tenmile Creek. Turn left after this bridge to continue south on the path. Remember that this path is paved over the old Colorado & Southern Railroad. Shortly after walking south, you will notice a large grassy opening to your right. This once served as the Frisco passenger depot for the Colorado & Southern. Above the old depot site, a large grey tailing pile can be seen. This once served as the Frisco Tunnel and was in operation until the 1930s. To the right of the Frisco Tunnel is also the Meridian Mine, owned by the Recen family, and a powder magazine, which was a room used to store black powder or dynamite. Due to its proximity, it is assumed that the Recens used this powder magazine for their mines on Mount Royal.

A group of passengers waits outside the train depot in Frisco.
(Frisco Historic Park & Museum)

Continue south down the path until you reach the Mount Royal Trailhead, at coordinates 39°34'21.1"N - 106°06'16.3"W.

Note the Forest Service trail signage and any trail or condition updates that they have posted, and then begin hiking up the Mount Royal Trail. Be mindful of other hikers on this trail, and as always, follow the proper trail and Leave-No-Trace etiquette. As you make your way uphill, stay to the right of any forks that split the main trail.

Colorado & Southern Locomotive plows snow from rails, 1898-1903.
(Park County Local History Digital Archive)

While hiking up the old route to work for many Masontown miners that lived in Frisco, make yourself available to the views of the town and Lake Dillon to your east. The valley where Lake Dillon sits is the convergence of three rivers, the Ten Mile, the Snake, and the Blue. Before the completion of the reservoir in 1963, this valley was where the old town sites of Dillon and Dickey sat. Owned by the Denver Water Board, Lake Dillon is the largest reservoir under their holding. The water is transported under the Continental Divide for 23.3 miles through the Harold D. Roberts Tunnel, which was named after a water rights attorney for the City of Denver. Mountains Grays and Torreys are the two largest peaks in sight, sitting off in the distance behind the lake. Both of these mountains reach elevations over 14,000 feet, with Torreys to the left from this view and Grays to the right.

Along the trail, you will notice plenty of flora and signs of fauna. Of the possible plants and wildlife to see, several are mentioned in the following pages. (Continues on p. 77)

Quaking Aspen:

While hiking, you will observe plenty of aspen trees. They can be identified by their tall, white bark, with dark markings similar to eyes. Quaking aspens are found from an elevation of 5,000 to 11,500 feet, placing them just at tree line. A group of aspen trees is called a "stand," and is one living organism connected by their roots underground. To help with their growth of population, aspens can clone themselves, with the clone growing alongside the parent tree from its roots.

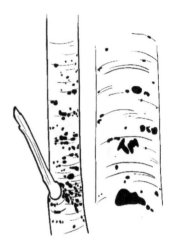

The bark on aspens will scar over any scratches or marks that damage the tree.

The leaf of an Aspen.

Unlike other deciduous trees, aspens grow year-round, even under the snow. In the summer, their leaves are bright green and offer a glitter-like appearance when blowing in the wind. In the fall, they turn to a golden yellow. Dryer, sunny seasons increase the sugar in the tree, resulting in brighter colors. To protect them from UV rays at this elevation, their bark produces a white powder, which shields the trunk from the direct sunlight. This powder can be taken off the tree with your hand and used as sunscreen, although it is only equal to about three SPF.

Evergreen Trees:

There are many forms of evergreen trees on Mount Royal. Of them are the Engelmann and Colorado spruce (the state tree), and the lodgepole, limber, and bristlecone pine. These trees thrive in this environment as they are comfortable with colder weather and take advantage of the snowmelt-producing wet soil. The Rocky Mountain juniper, found on the top of Mount Royal entering the scree fields, is native to Colorado; however, it is not native to this elevation. They found their way to the tree line and continue to grow here since they do not require much soil moisture, can withstand cold temperatures and can grow in rocky/sandy soil.

Colorado Spruce have waxy blueish-green needles.

Needles on a Lodgepole Pine grow in pairs of two, and are usually 1 ½" to 2 ½" inches long.

While the deciduous trees of Frisco will lose their leaves throughout the winter, the evergreen trees keep most of their shape and needles throughout all four seasons. A growing threat to these trees is the Mountain Pine Beetle, which burrows in the trunk, interrupting the movement of food for the tree, and eventually results in death.

Wildflowers:

The hike to and around Masontown offers visitors a chance to see many beautiful wildflowers from spring to fall. Given the time of year, you may see flowers such as alpine forget-me-nots or subalpine larkspurs. A common wildflower to see on this hike is the black-eyed Susan, with its yellow petals and dark center. Being a daisy-like flower, they will bloom in August and September.

Black-eyed Susans.

Colorado's state flower, the Colorado columbine, will be found blooming on this trail from spring to early summer. Their purple sepals and white center pedals stand out amongst the green and assist with spotting this flower. In 1899, Colorado adopted this as their state flower, and then in 1925, a law was passed to protect the flower. This law, which is still active today, made the uprooting of a columbine flower on public lands illegal.

Black-eyed Susan.

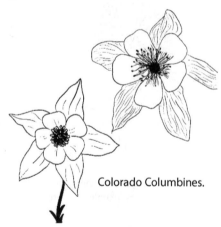

Colorado Columbines.

Moose:

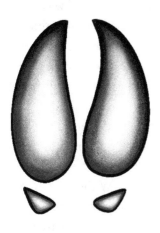

While moose are a common sight in Frisco, they are not native to this area. They were introduced for permanent population in Colorado in the late 1970s and have thrived ever since. They are large, fast, territorial animals, and will mark their territory by scraping trees with their antlers. If you see an aspen tree having the bark stripped off with scraping marks, it is likely that a moose shedding its antlers used this tree. A full-grown male moose will average six to seven feet tall at the shoulders and weigh around 1,000 pounds. They shed their antlers in late fall/early winter and regrow them in early spring.

Moose scat, similar in shape to elk scat, tells us and other animals where moose have been. It appears almost as a sawdust material once dried and broken apart. Moose tracks look similar to that of a white-tail deer, with an exception of track size, as they are both hooved mammals and members of the Cervidae family. Mule deer tracks, however, appear different, as these deer barely show the back two knuckles that a moose does.

Moose scat will change size and color with the seasons, as their diet consists of fresh growth in spring and summer.

Black Bear:

Although they are called black bears, these animals can be colored from shades of honey to black. The nickname "black bear" was given to the Ursus Americanus genus and species when first encountered in the Appalachian region, where most resemble more of a true black color. As opportunistic omnivores, black bears eat mostly forgeable items, but will occasionally eat scavenged animals. They will travel within a range of forty miles from their den in search of food.

While other types of bears may wander to border areas of Colorado in their feeding grounds, black bears are the only ones to populate the state. The average male size is three by five feet while on all fours, with an average weight nearing 500 pounds. While they do not truly hibernate, they go into what is called torpor. These bears will "den" from November to May, since their food sources are scarce during these months. The speed of a lean black bear not preparing for torpor can reach up to 30 miles per hour. Their tracks can be noticed both on the ground and in trees. However, tree markings appear only as the claw marks, left by the bear climbing up the tree.

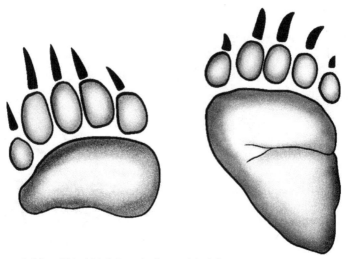

Front (left) and hind (right) tracks from a black bear.

(Continued from p. 71)

After remaining right at every fork of the main trail, you will arrive at coordinate's 39°33'57.6"N 106°06'07.6"W. Welcome to Masontown. Refer back to the chapter *In With the New* to look at the old photo of town from this vantage point, with the trail serving as Masontown's one street. One major difference between then and now, aside from the vanished buildings, is the density of forest. The mining industry required vast amounts of timber to build out mine frames, buildings, and to be used as fuel. This led to massive deforestation, with the trees only now on their way to regaining the land. While exploring, remember to leave all artifacts where you find them, as we wish to preserve what remains for future generations to experience.

When first arriving at the old site of the town, there will be a large clearing, with some downed logs perfect for benches. As you look around this area you will notice a large grey tailing pile to the right of the uphill trail. While looking at the tailing piles around the area, it can be determined what they mined for in that adit from the color of the pile. Due to the contents of certain ore carrying different metals, yellow tailings are a sign of gold mining, while grey tailings are heavier in galena, returning more lead or silver. Also noticeable at the entrance to town are several sunken pits in the ground. These are the remains of dugout sections for crawl spaces/cellars underneath the long-gone work sheds and buildings.

As you continue further uphill, scattered metal artifacts will begin to appear. After the slide of 1926, these artifacts were spread all throughout town, leading to their initial haphazard placement along the trail, which has been only further worsened by people interfering with their found locations. On the left of the trail is a tangled pile of rusted steel bindings. Opposite the trail of these bindings, an old rusted axel is found just off the path.

On each side of the trail, brick foundations will be found, with some remaining more intact than others. Using the photo of Masontown from earlier, along with other town photos in the *For What it is Named* chapter, you can see which building originally sat over which foundation. To the left of the trail uphill, there are many decimated foundations appearing as piles of brick, while on the right is a well-preserved brick foundation. This brick platform offers views of its wall to the back and has metal dowels stemming from the base. It is believed that this foundation housed a boiler, with the metal poles to hold it in place.

Behind this foundation, there is a crawl pit to the old building. Inside this impression of the ground, there are several metal remains, which appear to be old tin roofing. To the farthest back of the impression and slightly uphill, the only remaining wall of the town is found. Being roughly six feet by six feet, this wall most likely came from a section of the mill, as it is located in the ditch behind the mill grade.

Continuing uphill, the last major stop to the old town is on the right-hand side above a yellow tailing pile. This is the site of the Masontown Mill, which had been rebuilt, relocated, and renamed many times. If you continue up the path just shortly beyond the tailing, it will open up to the right of the trail, allowing you to walk onto the large grade for the mill. With a sizable flat portion, this is a great gauge to the dimensions of the mill that continuously operated here.

If you continue uphill above the mill site, there will be a steeper grade on the trail going nearly 150 feet until it turns right at coordinates 39°33'52.3"N 106°06'18.0"W. This viewpoint offers the same angle as the photo of the unknown man standing above the mill in the *For What it is Named* chapter. To the left, (uphill) of this area, the trail meets the remaining avalanche scar, where the 1926 slide entered the town.

From here, you may choose to continue up Mount Royal. If you do so, remember that it will be roughly 1,000 feet elevation gain in one mile. This is also an out and back trail and will have you backtrack the same way to where you began. Another option if you wish to continue hiking would be to take one of the two side trails that split from the town heading southeast. These trails will shortly meet up and take you to Rainbow Lake, roughly one mile away. This lake offers more views of the flora and fauna of Frisco and will have a trail straight from the lake to where the Recreation Path meets Second Avenue (a one-mile trail). While hiking around the Mount Royal/ Peak One area, you may see different cabin ruins and mining entrances. Due to the amount of claims on Mount Royal and this face of the range, it cannot be determined if they were associated with this property or belonged to one of the many other Frisco area claims. If you have had your share of hiking for the day, you can return to the parking lot by reversing the route that brought you to Masontown.

Map to Masontown:

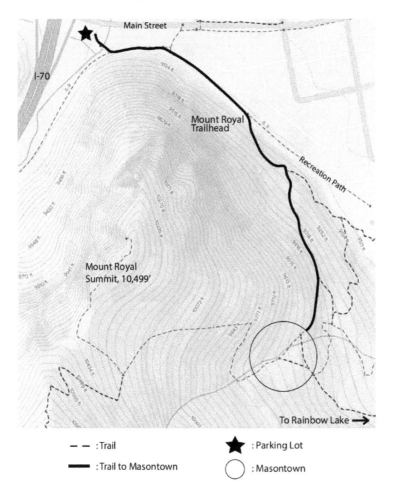

Claims Map

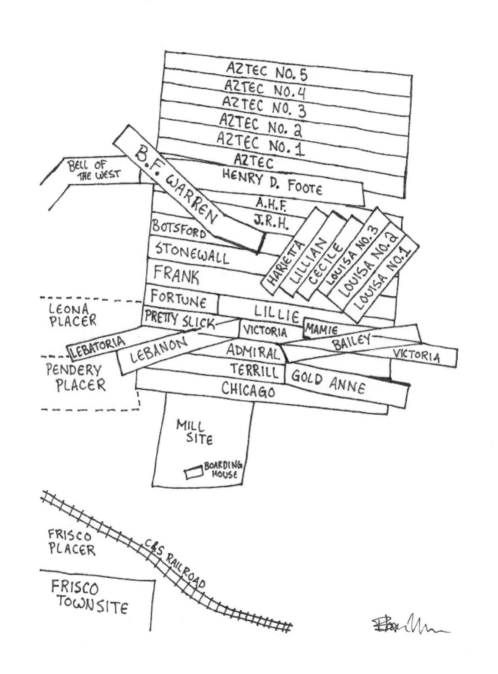

Glossary of Mining Terms

Adit: A horizontal entrance to a mine.

Agitation: Being stirred or shaken mechanically.

Amalgam: A combination of chemical and metal.

Amalgamation: The use of mercury or other chemicals to attract crushed gold and combine it with an amalgam.

Amend: To renew a mining claim.

Arrastra: A milling device that would crush and pulverize ores as they are dragged along the bottom of the cylinder.

Assaying: A test to determine the levels of valuable metal in an ore.

Bedrock: A layer of solid rock underneath soil.

Chute: A sloped path in which ore moves.

Claim: A section of land, usually 1,500 feet long, sold for the intent of mining.

Claim Jumping: Unlawful mining of a previously located claim.

Concentrate: A powder byproduct of milling, high in percentage of the desired metal.

Consolidation: The combination of claims previously owned by separate entities.

Crosscut: A level driven across a vein.

Crusher: A machine that reduces large rock into smaller pieces.

Cyanidation: A chemical method used to remove silver and gold from ore.

Cyanide: A chemical high in carbon and nitrogen that is used to dissolve silver and gold from ore.

Dissolution: The dismantling of a company or partnership.

District: A larger area of land designated and determined by the miners and minerals within them.

Drift: An underground, horizontal passage.

High-grade Ore: Ore that is above 20 ounces of desired metal per ton.

Hoist: A machine used for raising and lowering in a shaft.

Incorporation: Creation of a company or partnership.

Interests: A persons share of a mining claim, patent, or company.

Level: A tunnel cut from a main shaft. A drift.

Locate: To establish rights to a claim.

Lode: A metallic vein.

Low-grade Ore: Ore that is below 20 ounces of desired metal per ton.

Messrs.: Addressing several members of a firm, company, or partnership.

Mill: A plant in which ore is treated.

Mine: An excavation in the earth for minerals.

Mineral: A naturally occurring substance that could have monetary value.

Mining Application: A request for approval on a mining claim or patent.

Ore: A mixture of minerals that a metal can be extracted from.

Oxidizing: A chemical reaction that takes place when minerals are exposed to oxygen, which would break down the ore.

Patent: A mining claim where the land title is passed from the government to the claimant.

Placer: Sand or gravel that contained valuable minerals, easily mined by washing with water.

Precipitates: Dissolved minerals that are freed from a liquid, forming a deposit.

Pulp: A pulverized ore in solution.

Race: An open channel that carries water.

Reduction: To reduce the minerals in ore, leaving behind the desired metals.

Relocate: The purchase or location of an existing claim by a new entity.

Shaft: An inclined excavation, usually framed with wood.

Smelting: Reducing ores to metals in a furnace.

Solution: When an ore is mixed with a liquid to help extract metals.

Stamp: A machine for crushing ore.

Stamp Mill: A mill that utilizes stamps as the method for extracting metals from ore.

Strike: Finding valuable minerals.

Tailings: Gravel, dirt, and rocks, left behind from an excavation.

Tailing Pile: A pile of gravel, dirt, and rocks that stem from a mine entrance.

Tramway: A set of rails that direct a cart.

Tunnel: A horizontal underground passage, usually open on both ends.

Turbine: A wheel that is spun to produce power.

Undercut: To excavate under a determined body of ore.

Unwater: To free a mine of its water by draining or pumping.

Vein: A gathering of mineral matter in cracks or faults of rock.

Wildcat Mine: A mine prospected in an area not known to be productive.

Winze: A shaft that connects different levels.

Timeline of the Masontown Property

1866

- ☐ March 27- Federal Union Mining Company, based out of Idaho Springs, is incorporated. General Napoleon Bonaparte Buford is elected as the superintendent.
- ☐ September- Victoria Mine near Idaho Springs opened by Buford.
- ☐ The Buford Mill is opened next to the Victoria mine.

1867

- ☐ Spring- Buford is let go from his position with the Federal Union Mining Company due to negligent management of mines.

1869

- ☐ The camp surrounding Buford's Victoria mine in Idaho Springs is given the name Masonville.

1871

- ☐ January 3- The Franklin Company purchased the Victoria mine near Idaho Springs. They begin to rebuild over the old Buford Mill.

1880

- ☐ July 10- First newspaper reporting of the Victoria mine near Frisco.
- ☐ August 14- Alex C. Graff, William M. Graff, and William McNair begin looking at mines to invest in near Frisco.
- ☐ September 15- Messrs. Graff, Graff, and McNair incorporate Royal Mountain Mining and Milling Company.
- ☐ September 25- Graff and Mr. Pendery incorporate 18 claims on Royal Mountain, including the Victoria.

1881

- ☐ Royal Mountain M. & M. Co. has the first recorded stamp mill operating on this property.

- ☐ The Federal Silver Mining Company is incorporated, with J.F. Keifer as President, alongside partners Henry Foote and Mr. Warren.

- ☐ March 11- The main tunnel of Royal Mountain M & M Co. is 130 feet deep.

- ☐ May 21- Graff purchased 160 acres surrounding the Victoria.

- ☐ May 28- Graff purchases the Pendery Placer, sitting just beside the mill site.

- ☐ October 21- James McWalters is murdered at the Morrow S.S. Saloon in Frisco.

1882

- ☐ Alex C. Graff is serving as Mayor of Frisco as well as heading the Victoria mine.

- ☐ The Denver & Rio Grande Railroad opens in Frisco.

- ☐ September- Federal Silver Mining Company locates the Bailey, B.F. Warren, and Henry D. Foote lodes, including 5.17 acres on Mount Royal.

1883

- ☐ Royal Mountain M. & M. Co. is still operating this mine, but have closed their mill.

- ☐ The Denver South Park & Pacific Railroad opens in Frisco.

- ☐ April 7- General Napoleon Bonaparte Buford dies in Chicago.

1885

- ☐ Royal Mountain M. & M. Co. ceases operations.

- ☐ Hathaway and Lamping open their kilns along the DSP&PRR outside of Frisco.

1887

☐ Lars Matsson moves to the United States from Sweden.

1892

☐ Federal Silver Mining Co. amends location of Henry D. Foote lode.

1894

☐ Alex C. Graff dies in Routt County, Colorado.

☐ Lars Matsson is working as a mining contractor in Frisco with partner Recen.

☐ Lars Matsson is working as a mining broker in Frisco with partner Engstrom.

1898

☐ Lars Matsson is the sole owner of the Victoria group of mines.

☐ August 11- Pug Ryan and his band of outlaws rob the Denver Hotel in Breckenridge.

☐ November 12- Frank T. Botsford et al locate the Frank and Pretty Slick lodes.

☐ November 20- Messrs. Edwin Hall, Frank Olson, and Mr. Smith lease the Victoria group from Matsson for $20,000.

☐ December 24- Large gold strike at the Victoria returning $40-250 a ton. Frisco fills up all lodging with miners coming to work the strike.

1899

☐ Oliver Swanson builds his saloon at the corner of Second Avenue and Main Street.

☐ January 14- Plans begin for a new reduction plant for the Victoria.

☐ January 21- Hall is made manager, and Olson made superintendent. Ore is being processed at the Smith-Olson Mill just north of town. Capt. T.A. Brown purchases a ¼ stake in the Victoria property.

- ☐ February 4- Snow slide hits the mouth of the Victoria mine and destroys the road to the railroad.

- ☐ March 4- Victoria is back to regular shipments after the slide.

- ☐ April 15- John D. Hynderliter opens six claims above the Victoria.

- ☐ May 6- Hall and Olson open a new body of ore above the Victoria.

- ☐ August 26- Frank T. Botsford sues to Federal Silver Mining Company over claimed abandonment of the Bailey lode.

- ☐ December 25- The newly erected Town Hall opens in Frisco.

1900

- ☐ January 27- Matsson and a partner are working the upper levels of the Victoria group. New lessee's E.W. Hallen and Kogsberg are working the lower portion.

- ☐ February 24- Matsson is developing the mill site in preparation for a sale to Mr. Person, of St Louis. Included in this sale is six mining claims near the Victoria, owned by Frisco Mayor Harry Britton.

- ☐ February 24- Frank Judson and Victoria Judson deed all interest to Frank T. Bosford for the Botsford, Stonewall, Frank, Pretty Slick, Adelaide, Terrell, Victoria, and Victoria mill site.

- ☐ May 5- John B. Killgore deeds interest to Frank T. Botsford for the Bailey, Henry D Foote, and B.F. Warren lodes.

1901

- ☐ The school board purchases the old Swanson Saloon from Mr. Schloss and begins holding class as the new schoolhouse.

1902

- ☐ February 15- Matsson is finalizing deal of the Victoria group to Mr. Person.

- ☐ June 7- Frank Olson and Frank B. Wiborg purchase 1,500

linear feet of the Mamie and Lillie lodes.

- ☐ August 23- Frank T. Botsford sold all of his interests in the B. F. Warren and Henry D. Foote lodes to Abel H. Frost. Frost then transferred his claims to these lodes along with his personal claims of the Frank and Botsford lodes to his company, the Admiral Gold Mining Company, with partner E. E. Busby.

- ☐ December 13- Mr. Person forfeits claim back to Matsson. Matsson begins process of adding a lower adit.

1903

- ☐ March 14- Matsson reduces workforce and begins exploring across the veins.

- ☐ October 10- A. E. Keables travels from Denver to Frisco to inspect mines. Accompanying him is his partner, an expert mill man, from Masontown, Pennsylvania.

- ☐ October 17- William Staley hauls 45 wagonloads of materials to the Victoria Mill from the Wilson Smelter. Materials are used for mill improvements.

- ☐ September- The Masontown Mining and Milling Company is incorporated and capitalized at $1,500,000 (worth $45,000,000 today). J.V. Hoover is president, Silas R. Provins is treasurer, and A. E. Keables is secretary.

- ☐ September 26- Masontown M. & M. Co. purchases the Victoria group from Matsson for $25,000.

- ☐ October 10- Masontown M. & M. Co. purchases the Smith-Olson Mill to be reassembled at the Victoria Mill site. George Wortman, of the Climax Mine, supervises the moving and reconstruction.

- ☐ November 7- Hoover announces that the new mill will be 50x140 feet, including twenty stamps with cyanide attachments.

- ☐ December 12- Masontown is working all available men.

1904

- March 22- Lars Matsson dies of pneumonia.
- June 1- The new Masontown Mill opens.
- June 11- A. E. Keables is promoted to superintendent of the company. David H. Lawrence is elected as superintendent of the mill, along with Frank Graham elected as company assayer. Masontown now consists of 12 lode claims, one placer claim, one mill, and roughly 100 acres.
- July 4- J.V. Hoover organized a Fourth of July Picnic at Masontown. George and Lillie Wortman, now running the Masontown Boarding house, served the picnic.

1905

- Masontown halts work for most of the year due to ownership arguments.
- January 7- Admiral Gold Mining Company amends partial ownership of Pretty Slick and Victoria lodes, and the Victoria Mill.
- May 13- J.V. Hoover travels east in attempt to settle ownership affairs.
- July 1- Keables begins work on the mill so that the company can mine in full force when work resumes.
- August 26- Masontown M. & M. Co. files suit for liberation.
- October 14- Company investors now rightfully own Masontown M. & M. Co. Work resumes on the Victoria.
- December 16- Keables and Lawrence begin installing a hoisting plant.

1906

- February 10- Matsson's will deeds Masontown property to Hoover and Provins. Dan Recen sues the company for a $2,500 commission of sale.

- ☐ October- George D. Hibbs visits Frisco from Pennsylvania to look over the Victoria mine.
- ☐ October 20- J. Percy Hart is hired as manager of operations. He, along with his wife and three kids, move to a cabin on the Masontown Property.
- ☐ October 31- Hibbs Mining and Milling Company is incorporated.
- ☐ November- Masontown Mining and Milling Company has abruptly dissolved.
- ☐ November- The Hibbs Mining and Milling Company has taken over operations of the Masontown Property.
- ☐ December 15- Admiral Gold Mining Co. buys the Terrill, Admiral, and Chicago lodes.

1907

- ☐ The Hibbs Mining and Milling Company is now operating the Victoria group and mill, working three shifts of men.
- ☐ February 18- Hibbs M. & M. Co. has their first sizable strike on the property. J. Percy Hart is still heading operations.
- ☐ April 6- The Aztec Mining and Milling Company purchases claims from the Admiral Gold Mining Company. They then locate and begin mining the Aztec 1-5 lodes, further above the Victoria.
- ☐ April 7- Keables and Lawrence are arrested for mail fraud regarding their involvement with the Lost Bullions Spanish Mine.
- ☐ July 20- Hart has cut the main tunnel 500 feet deeper in preparation for a lower adit that will exit the mine level with the railroad.
- ☐ August 25- Keables and Lawrence are sentenced to fifteen days in jail and a $500 fine for their association with the Lost Bullion Spanish Mine.

- [ ] <u>September 6</u>- William Graff dies in Dillon, Colorado.
- [ ] <u>December 21</u>- J. Percy Hart starts up a monthly newsletter titled *The Successful Miner*.

1908

- [ ] J. Percy Hart is now serving as mayor of Frisco along with manager of the Victoria.
- [ ] Dr. A.W. Clark, of Omaha, is serving as president of the Hibbs M. & M. Co.
- [ ] <u>January 18</u>- J.V. Hoover dies in his hometown of Masontown, Pennsylvania.
- [ ] <u>April 25</u>- Hart begins raising money to improve the mill.
- [ ] <u>October 16</u>- William H Staley dies in a freighting accident outside of Frisco.

1909

- [ ] <u>October 9</u>- Hart writes a letter to George Robinson demonstrating financial troubles of the company. He asked Robinson not to publish Hibbs' delinquent taxes in the upcoming newspaper.
- [ ] <u>November 6</u>- Hart is elected as treasurer, and secretary of Hibbs M. & M. Co., along with his previous titles of manager and town mayor. Hart travels east to negotiate for a new oxidizing method to be installed in the mill.

1910

- [ ] <u>July 23</u>- Dr. A.W. Clark along with Hibbs investors Rev. Warren P. Clark and R.E. Stewart come to town to check on the mine and find great conditions. J. Percy Hart has installed a new 65-foot winze.
- [ ] <u>December 17</u>- Dissolution of the Aztec Mining Company takes place.
- [ ] <u>December 20</u>- The Frisco Mining, Milling, and Discover Company is incorporated, headed by J. Percy Hart.

1911

- Frisco Mining, Milling, and Development Company acquires the John D. Hynderliter claims, above the Victoria, and plans to purchase thirty more claims on Mount Royal.

- Hart publishes *An Effectual Remedy for the Evils in Mining and Mining Companies,* a 32-page pamphlet outlining the intentions of the Frisco Mining, Milling, and Development Company for investors.

- Hart is secretary, manager, and treasurer of the Frisco M. M. & D. Co., alongside company president John W. Lynn, of Omaha.

- April- Last reported workings of the Hibbs M & M Co, stating that they drove a 100 winze and that their cyanide treatment was not yielding the best results.

- May 27- Consolidation of the mining claims adjoining the Victoria takes place.

- December 11- Final verdict is served after appeals on the Lost Bullion Spanish Mine case, resulting in Keables and Lawrence paying their fines and jail sentence.

1912

- January 27- Old Masontown property is relocated and now being worked by the Frisco M. M. & D. Co., along with their four Hynderliter claims. Hart is Manager and Frank Cherry-holmes is superintendent.

- January 27- Work is being done to push past a cave in on the Lebanon Lode.

- June 21- Hart and Frederick William Echternkamp travel together to Breckenridge to discuss business.

- July 12- Echternkamp is hired by the Frisco M. M. & D. Co. to get the property back into working order.

1913

☐ Dissolution of the Frisco Mining Milling & Development Company takes place.

☐ April 5- All mining claims, equipment, and buildings of the old Hibbs Mining and Milling Company, most recently owned by the Frisco M. M. & D. Co., goes on auction. Echternkamp purchases these claims and buildings.

1914

☐ June 4- Someone steals the door from the Victoria Mill.

☐ June 12- Ed Huter helps Echternkamp clean up a cave in of the Victoria mine.

☐ October 9- The Frisco M. M. & D. Co. sues Echternkamp.

☐ October 30- Vandalism takes place on the Echternkamp property, smashing his mill windows and destroying mining equipment.

1915

☐ Hibbs M. & M. Co. is listed as a defunct Colorado mining company.

☐ June 26- Echternkamp hits bedrock and believes to be in the ore he wants shortly.

1916

☐ October 23- Newspaper reports of Echternkamp mining this area, along with his large plant, machinery, and mill.

1918

☐ November 6- Echternkamp purchases a ranch in Craig, Colorado, and moves here with his family. He leaves his mining of the Victoria behind.

1920

☐ July 4- David H. Lawrence dies in Denver, Colorado.

1922

☐ Echternkamp dies at his ranch in Craig, Colorado.

1926

☐ <u>May 19</u>- A large snow slide hits the Masontown property and covers the C. & S. railroad tracks beneath. All that is left at the Masontown property is one cabin and brick foundations.

1927

☐ <u>February 8</u>- Albert Elisha Keables dies and is buried in Sacramento, California.

1947

☐ <u>February 27</u>- J. Percy Hart dies in Los Angeles, California.

1963

☐ The Frisco Schoolhouse holds its last class.

1968

☐ The Forest Service determines the ruins of Masontown a forest fire risk. They are removed through a controlled burn.

About the Author

Blair Miller is a historian, woodworker, and nature enthusiast who lives in Frisco, Colorado. He began working in the museum field while receiving a degree in Public History and Museum Studies from Central Michigan University. Since his graduation, Blair has worked in both traditional and children's museums, specializing in education, exhibit design, and research. When he is not working at the Frisco Historic Park & Museum, you can find him playing music and spending time outdoors. To see more of Blair's public history work, visit Blairfmiller.com.

About the Frisco Historic Park & Museum

The Frisco Historic Park & Museum was founded in 1983 by a group of women and men who saw value in historic preservation and sought to collect, preserve, and present the story of Frisco. The Historic Park & Museum now features ten historic cabins and buildings with year-round exhibits, guided tours, a robust archive and collection, educational programming, and much more. It is through the generosity of the Frisco community that the Historic Park & Museum is able to dedicate the resources to research and writing under the Frisco Historic Park & Museum Press.

The Frisco Historic Park & Museum seeks to preserve and promote the Town of Frisco's heritage and history by presenting an excellent educational museum experience to the community and its visitors.

Scan this QR code to learn more about the Frisco Historic Park & Museum, and the history of Frisco, Colorado.

Bibliography

"All Eyes Turned Towards Frisco." *Summit County Journal*, January, 1899.

Allegheny Cemetery, Pittsburgh, Allegheny County, Pennsylvania, USA. Alexander Graff. Section 16 Lot 1.

Allegheny Cemetery, Pittsburgh, Allegheny County, Pennsylvania, USA. William Graff. Section 16 Lot 1.

Barnard, A.W. "Bullion Reports and Mining Items." *Colorado Miner*, January, 1871.

Beall, W.T. "Mining Application No. 5429." *Summit County Journal*, June, 1902.

Beall, W.T. "Mining Application No. 5823." *Summit County Journal*, November, 1906.

Beall, W.T. "Mining Application No. 5826." *Summit County Journal*, December, 1906.

Beal, W.T. "Notice of Protest." *Summit County Journal*, August, 1899.

"*Breckenridge Bulletins*." *Breckenridge Bulletin*, December, 1907.

"Brought To Pay." *Summit County Journal*, May, 1902.

"Cases Docketed for District Court." *Summit County Journal*, October, 1914.

Colliers, *the National Weekly*. Volume XXXIX, July, 1907. Page 22.

Colorado State Archives. Secretary of State, Incorporation Record. October 31, 1906. S501, Book 121, Page 32.

Colorado State Archives. Secretary of State, Incorporation Record. September 15, 1880. S502, Book 4, Page 422.

Colorado State Business and Mines Directory, 1881, page 324

Colorado State Business and Mines Directory, 1883, page 341

Colorado State Business Directory, 1894, pages 468 and 814.

Craig Cemetery, Craig, Colorado, United States. Section F17, Plot 1.

"Critic's Letter." *Mining Investor*, April, 1907.

"Critic's Letter." *Mining Investor*, September, 1907.

Dempsey, Stanley. *Early Mining Law Matters: Ten Mile Mining District-Summit County, Colorado.* January 9, 1987

"Denver Hotel." *Summit County Journal*, December, 1898.

"Died." *Summit County Journal*, March, 1904.

"Died." *Summit County Journal*, September, 1907.

Engineering and Mining Journal 19070-1-26: Vol 83 Issue 4. Page 211.

Engineering and Mining Journal, July 1-December 31, 1906. Page 554.

Engineering and Mining Journal, July 1-December 31, 1915. Page 554.

Fairmount Cemetery, Denver, Colorado, United States. Memorial ID 123440272

"Filed for Record." *Summit County Journal*, August, 1902.

"Filed with the Recorder." *Breckenridge Bulletin*, May, 1900.

"Found in Frisco." *Summit County Journal* and *Breckenridge Bulletin*, July, 1910.

"The Fourth at Frisco." *Breckenridge Bulletin*, July, 1904.

"Frisco District." *Breckenridge Bulletin*, January, 1900.

"Frisco Flashes." *Summit County Journal* & *Breckenridge Bulletin*, July, 1912.

Frisco Historic Park & Museum, 86.1.52

Frisco Historic Park & Museum, 2009.10.31

Frisco Historic Park & Museum, 2009.10.33

Frisco Historic Park & Museum, 2016.10.11A-C

Frisco Historic Park & Museum, 2017.9.203

Frisco Historic Park & Museum, 2017.9.250

Frisco Historic Park & Museum, 2017.9.254

"Frisco Jottings." *Summit County Journal*, June, 1901.

"Frisco Mines." *Summit County Journal*, April, 1899.

"Frisco Side Lights." *Breckenridge Bulletin*, October, 1903.

"From the Records of Summit County." *Breckenridge Bulletin*, April, 1907.

Frost, A. H. "Notice of Dissolution." *Summit County Journal* and *Breckenridge Bulletin*, December, 1910.

Georgetown Miner. "Frisco Facts." *Leadville Weekly Democrat*, July, 1880.

Hart, J. Percy. *Hart's History and Directory of the Three Towns, Brownsville, Bridgeport, West Brownsville*, page 240. Cadwallader, Pennsylvania, 1904.

Henry, John H. "Mining Application 1180." *Colorado Miner*, May, 1881.

Hollister, Ovando J. *The Mines of Colorado*, Samuel Bowles & Company, 20th Edition, 1867. Pages 232 & 330.

Hollister, Ovando J. "Mining in Clear Creek County." *Daily Mining Journal*, September, 1866.

"In Mine and Mill." *Summit County Journal*, August 26, 1905.

J.H.M. "Frisco News." *Summit County Journal*, May, 1899.

"Jail Delivery." *Summit County Journal*, June, 1902.

"Judge Lewis Sentences Fake Mine Promoters." *San Francisco Call*, December, 1907.

"Kokomo Kodak's." *Breckenridge Bulletin*, July, 1902.

"Land Office." *Leadville Daily Herald*, September, 1882.

"Land Office Business." *Carbonate Chronicle*, September, 1883.

"Land Office Business." *Leadville Daily Herald*, December, 1882.

Library of Congress, LCB-814- 1547, Lot 4192

"Live News Noted from Busy Frisco." *Summit County Journal*, March 1915.

"Lost Bullion Spanish Mine." Golden Transcript, December, 1969.

"Masontown Starts Up." *Summit County Journal*, June, 1904.

Miller, E.J. Official Souvenir and Manual of the Fifteenth General Assembly of the State of Colorado. Denver, Colorado, 1905.

"Mining in Summit County." *Breckenridge Bulletin*, October, 1903.

"Mining in Summit County." *Breckenridge Bulletin*, December, 1903.

"Mining in Summit County." *Breckenridge Bulletin*, June, 1904.

"Mining Items." *Summit County Journal* and *Breckenridge Bulletin*, November 1909.

"Mining News." *Breckenridge Bulletin*, August, 1905.

"Mining News." *Summit County Journal*, October, 1903.

"Mining News." *Summit County Journal*, November, 1903.

"Mining Notes." *Leadville Weekly Herald*, April, 1881.

Mining Reporter, January 1- July 31, 1905. Page 197.

"Mischievous Boys at Mine Property." *Summit County Journal*, October, 1914.

"New Life at Frisco." *Breckenridge Bulletin*, June, 1907.

"New Mexico Mining Fraud Promoters are Convicted" *Roswell Daily Record*, August 1907.

"Northwestern Colorado." *Steamboat Pilot*, May, 1926.

Old Quartz. "Frisco." *Summit County Journal*, January, 1899.

Old Quartz. "Ore Worth from $40 to $250 a Ton." *Summit County Journal*, December, 1898.

"Our Chief Industry." *Summit County Journal*, October, 1906.

"Patents Received." *Herald Democrat*, May, 1892.

Rogers, Fred. "Frisco Items." *Colorado Miner*, August, 1880.

School of Mines, Quarterly, April, 1911.

Secretary of State. "New Business Enterprises." *Union Labor Bulletin*, December, 1910.

"Shot Dead in Quarrel." *San Juan Prospector*, April, 1908.

Southern Methodist University, Federal Union Mining Company Records, a Guide to the Collection.

"Staley Crushes Skull." *Summit County Journal*, October, 1908.

"Sues for Commission." *Summit County Journal*, February, 1906.

"Summit County." *Leadville Daily Herald*, February, 1882.

Summit County Journal, December, 1905.

"Ten Mile Notes." *Leadville Weekly Democrat*, February, 1881.

"Ten Mile Notes." *Leadville Weekly Democrat*, March, 1881.

Thomas, Walter R. "Sheriff's Sale." *Summit County Journal* and *Breckenridge Bulletin*, March, 1913.

"Thriving Frisco Mines." *Summit County Journal*, May 1905.

United States Census, Frisco, Precinct 7, Summit County, Colorado, 1900.

United States Census, Frisco, Precinct 7, Summit County, Colorado, 1910.

United States Census, Frisco, Precinct 7, Summit County, Colorado, 1930.

United States Census, Los Angeles, Assembly District 72, Los Angeles, California, 1920.

United States Census, Los Angeles, Los Angeles, California, 1930.

United States Census, Los Angeles, Los Angeles, California, 1940.

United States Census, Miller, District 0121, Knox, Nebraska, 1910.

United States Death Index, California, 1940-1997.

"Victoria Group Sold." *Breckenridge Bulletin*, February, 1900.

"Victoria Sold Again." *Summit County Journal*, September 1903.

Weiser, R. "Masonville Reduction Works." *Colorado Miner*, April, 1873.

"Wireless Grams from Frisco." *Summit County Journal* and *Breckenridge Bulletin*, January 1912.

The World To-day (Chicago, The World To-day Company, 1907). Pages 1231-1234.

Index

A

B

C

D

E

F

Leyner Hotel 10, 11, 15
Leyner, Peter 10, 11
Lost Bullion Spanish Mine Company 45
Lynn, John W. 52, 54

M

Mason, A. S. 6
Masontown 1-3, 5-7, 18, 19, 33-41, 43, 44, 46-48, 55, 57-59, 61, 63, 66
Masontown Mining and Milling Company 1, 33
(see also) Masontown M. & M. Co. 33-36, 39-41, 43, 46, 47
Matsson, Lars 24, 28, 33, 34, 35, 39, 40
McNair, William 17
McWalters, James 12-14, 88
Moonshiners 2, 62, 63
Morrow S. S. Saloon 12-15
Mount Royal 1, 3, 18, 19, 26, 51, 55, 57, 61, 63, 66

O

Olson, Frank 24, 25, 34

P

Pendery, J.L. 18, 87, 88
Prohibition 62
Provins 34, 35, 39

R

Recen, Daniel 40
Recen, Henry 40
Robinson, George B. 47, 48
Royal Mountain Mining Company 18-22
Ryan, "Pug" 27, 28

S

Smith, Mr. 24, 25, 28, 34, 35, 89, 91
Smith-Olson Mill, 25 91
(See also) Smith-Olson Stamp Mill 34
Summit County 5, 10, 13, 27, 36, 58, 62
Summit County Journal 25, 29, 35, 56
Swanson, Oliver 20, 29, 89, 90
Swanson Saloon 30

T

Tenmile Canyon 17, 45

U

Union Pacific Railroad 5

V

Victoria Mill 33-35, 40, 41, 43
Victoria Mountain 1, 57

W

Washington Mining & Milling Company 36
Whitney, Sumner, 27, 28
Whitney & Whiting Company 7
West Point Academy 3
Wiborg, Frank B. 32, 90

CPSIA information can be obtained
at www.ICGtesting.com
Printed in the USA
JSHW032234190622
27231JS00005B/29

THE STORY OF MASONTOWN, a ghost town on the outskirts of Frisco proper, has always been one of Frisco's most disputed histories. While different accounts of this mining camp offer opposing timelines and functions, this book stands as the first comprehensive narrative of Masontown from its puzzling origins to its devastating avalanche in the 1920s. The invigorating gold strikes at this Victoria Mine helped populate Frisco, with the largest strike resulting in no vacancy for all town lodging. Continued work in search of pay ore at the Victoria resulted in dozens of important townsfolk moving to the area, including early mayors and sheriffs.

Established concurrently with Frisco's town charter, Masontown held space for the scandals, crimes, and riches of early Colorado boomtowns such as lawsuits, fraud, robbery and murder, claim jumping, and moonshining. While hikers today pass by the old tailing piles and brick foundations of what once sat overlooking the Mount Royal Trail, and this book includes a hiking guide to visit these sites and understand the trials and tribulations that took place. Along with never before published photographs, maps, and journals, this clearing of Masontown's rubble relay the importance behind this camp and its direct ties to Frisco as a town and mining operations in Summit County as a whole.

Previously unpublished maps, photographs, and illustrations!

FRISCO HISTORIC PARK AND MUSEUM PRESS
120 E. Main Street
Frisco, Colorado 80443

ISBN 978-1-943829-44-6
90000
9 781943 829446